THE LONG LINE

Three Plays by

Tom Hadaway

———

This edition first published 1994 by IRON Press, 5 Marden Terrace, Cullercoats, North Shields, Northumberland NE30 4PD, UK. Tel: 091 253 1901.

Typeset in Palatino 10pt. by Roger Booth Associates, Half Moon Chambers, 10 The Bigg Market, Newcastle upon Tyne NE1 1UW. Tel: 091 232 8301.

Printed by The Print House, Unit 5, Prospect Terrace, North Shields, Tyne & Wear NE30 1DX. Tel: 091 258 7027.

ISBN 0 90 6228-43-3.

IRON Press gratefully acknowledges the financial assistance of Northern Arts.

With thanks to Max Roberts of Live Theatre for photographs and other assistance.

IRON Press books are represented by:
Password Books Ltd
23 New Mount Street
Manchester M4 4DE
Tel: 061 953 4009
Fax: 061 953 4001

Contents

Foreword

TOM HADAWAY'S first produced play was *A Quaker in Cullercoats*, at Newcastle's People's Theatre in 1972. This followed the broadcast of some of his stories on BBC Radio 4 (or was it then still the Home Service?). The late playwright C.P. Taylor heard the first story, *The One That Got Away*, liked it and shoved a note through Hadaway's door telling him he should think of writing drama (Taylor was to prove the man's great mentor).

Praise was unlikely to go to Hadaway's head; the reaction of the Newcastle Journal theatre critic, Stanley Hurwitz to *Quaker* was to call it "nothing but a basket of red herrings. Hadaway is attempting to paint with oils when he has not yet mastered crayons", wrote Hurwitz.

Writers who survive this kind of critical baptism usually do well, and again encouraged by Taylor (who told him he should learn from the criticism rather than dismiss it), Hadaway buckled down for his second play, *God Bless Thee Jackie Maddison*, for BBC Television. It seemed the crayon box was laid aside – the play was chosen as a BAFTA entry.

Hadaway has been such a presence in North-East drama it's difficult to think he was virtually unknown twenty years ago, and that his writing didn't start until he was well into his forties.

He has now written ten stage plays, seven television plays, and three screenplays. Every stage play was for Newcastle's Live Theatre, every television play was for the BBC, and every screenplay was for Amber Films, Newcastle. This is a remarkable consistency. Hadaway is a man of place in more ways than one (he still lives close to North Shields where he was born).

After C.P. Taylor's death in 1981, it seemed natural that Tom Hadaway would become Live's new unofficial resident writer, and his relationship with director Max Roberts has proved extremely fruitful; their latest production happened in 1993, two powerful back-to-back short plays, *Seafarers*. Most – though not all – his plays involve themselves with Shields' fishing industry, the writer's most happy hunting ground, and one with which he is intimately familiar. The industry serves as a backdrop to each of the three plays published here, just as each, in its own way, charts the decline of fishing in Shields.

The Filleting Machine, which emerged as a stage play in the mid-seventies, ten years later was made into a feature film by that gutsy co-operative Amber Films. This was a landmark, for it marked not only the start of Amber's long association with North Shields, but also the first time they had ventured away from documentary into drama.

Time and Money appeared also in the seventies under its original title *The Pigeon Man*, while *The Long Line* toured with Live Theatre in 1986. The play's title has two meanings; it's both a conservation-conscious way of fishing, also the lineage of the fishing families whose history it charts.

It's significant that among all the huge changes of recent years in the North-East, Live Theatre Company has survived, Amber Films has survived, and Tom Hadaway has survived. Much recent 'community theatre' in this region (which spawned its growth in the 70s) has been imminently forgettable. Maybe the kind of Hadaway/Live Theatre partnership only happens occasionally, when the chemistry is right, for without doubt the opening of a new Hadaway play at that small Quayside theatre is always an eagerly awaited event.

The man has ploughed a highly individual furrow, surviving with a sense of dignity (he is now into his seventies) that filters through into his plays. The writing is often remarkable, simultaneously in touch with the everyday world of fisherfolk, or other working aspects of Tyneside, yet tinged with a powerful lyricism that can almost 'sing'.

An increasingly homogenised world tends to diminish an artist's sense of 'place', and indeed many modern artists, seeing the world itself as their subject matter, would scorn the very idea. The North-East itself, as it spawns the likes of Nissan, Metro Centre and other flash symbols of bland universality, has a shrinking generation of writers reflecting its deep–rooted character. C.P. Taylor managed it, despite being a native Glaswegian, also the late novelist Sid Chaplin. Catherine Cookson evokes a kind of nostalgic deprivation powerful in its own manner. Good modern playwrights such as Alex Ferguson, Michael Wilcox and Rod Wooden have all drawn convincingly on the region in different ways, but there is something about Tom Hadaway that marks him out from these, and I believe it is the channelling of his creativity into the very minutiae which formed him, a lifetime spent responding and reacting to an area and a style of life which throb through his plays like a fishing boat engine.

Which is not to deny his other achievements. *Yesterday's Children* is a play about prison life in Durham, which sprang from his writer's residency in three Durham jails (and his IRON Press book *Prison Writers*). *The Long Shadows* (co-written with his daughter, Pauline Hadaway) is an ambitious play about the South Shields man Ian Davidson imprisoned in Cyprus for murder after joining the PLO (his eventual release in 1993 attracted great publicity).

But we return to the Shields plays, to the fishing background. Because Hadaway's work speaks, without condescension, artifice or mannerism for a culture it knows intimately.

Like most North-East writers, his birthplace has worked against him, if universal acclaim is the yardstick. Posterity will, I hope, sort that out. I believe his stature will grow, because the plays themselves speak so powerfully and truthfully (they're often very funny too), and IRON Press is delighted to offer this threesome in print.

Read them, and – if you can – see them. It's real culture, not the kind of thing they force feed you at the Heritage Centres.

Peter Mortimer, Editor
IRON Press
Spring 1994

—— *Author's Note* ——

BORN ON WATERVILLE ROAD, North Shields and schooled at 'Ralphies' on the Ridges Estate, I left at 14 to end up on the fish quay. There I met pal and fellow fish filleter 'Muts' who would say wise/funny things like "There's two sorts of education! Sort the' keep for thorsel's an' the sort the' give to us". He could boast it took six polis's to bang him up, and he had the bruises to show, but a machine arrived that could cut fish faster than ten men, and this giant of a man was undermined. *The Filleting Machine* is his story, and of a Ridges family struggling against the odds, written before that estate's change of name to the Meadowell, and a quarter of a century before its riots brought ill famed prominence. Intellectuals told me 'it demonstrates the intrusion of economic forces into the lives of ordinary people'. I'd never thought of that, I just loved Muts, Ridges people and C. P. Taylor who advised me, 'write from your own back yard'.

In the same way, Arthur and Charlie in *Time and Money*, were two elderly working men I had daily contact with over twenty years. Trapped in the cheerless confine of a fish curing shed, their boss was the telephone on the wall, and they only had each other to complain to, or me if I happened to pop my head through the door. Arthur consoled himself with his love for racing pigeons which he kept up the bank. He could hold a bird comfortably in his hand as we sat talking in his allotment, and he would include it in the conversation. "Yor ma was a good'n eh! wasn't she?"

The Long Line spans a generation before I was born, but it is partly the story of my uncle George who was a coble fisherman, and said amazing things,

"Fish is like folks, the' live in toons an' villages, an' what they cannit abide is sudden disturbance".

It is also a story of hopes, dreams and love lost, but its conclusion comes inexorably to a boat bearing the name of a Shields boy, and his will to sail it forever.

Tom Hadaway, Spring 1994

─── *The Filleting Machine* ───

This play was first performed on stage by Live Theatre Company in the Central Club, North Shields in 1974.

Original Cast

Tom Hadaway   –   Father

Annie Orwin   –   Alice

Val McLane   –   Ma

Sammy Johnson   –   Davey

Directed by Murray Martin

The photograph shows Tom Hadaway and Val McLane in rehearsal.

CHARACTERS

MA	in her fifties
DA	also in his fifties
DAVY	15 their eldest son
ALICE	14 their eldest daughter

SCENE: A COUNCIL HOUSE LIVING ROOM, WITH KITCHEN
(Off stage. The house is on the Ridges estate, North Shields. The area is a depressed enclave of poor whites who have been slum-cleared from the fish dock district. In the distance, the raucous strident sound of children in the battlefield of the street can be heard.)

(MA is preparing a meal. ALICE calls from offstage)

ALICE   Mother! Mother!

MA   Hellow!

(The door opens and ALICE comes bursting in)

ALICE   The bairn's covered wi' baked beans, an' tea leaves.

MA   Gawd almighty!

ALICE   Tattie peelin's, an allsorts reet in the pram.

MA   That dorty buggar upstairs. Tossin' his rubbish oot the winder.

ALICE   It's all claggy. Yuk! *(She limps across the room. One of her legs is bandaged)*

MA   Tryin' ti get the dinner on. An' look at the state o' that bandage. Fresh on this mornin'. Ye'll end up with it septic.

ALICE   Better take a flannel, the pram's *lathered.*

(MA snatches a cloth from a drying line)

MA   Take that buggar a piece o' me mind *(She leaves and we hear her voice offstage, receding)* Ye great lazy good for nowt. Ye've got the place covered wi' yor filth.

(ALICE switches on her transistor radio. Music. She wanders over to the window to listen to the altercation outside)

Aye! thor's none so deef as doesn't want ti hear. Fancy hevin' ti live under dorty buggars like you.

(ALICE wanders back to a chair, sits and takes up a comic)

3

Ye want bloody sortin' out.

(The kitchen door opens and DAVY comes cautiously in. He is dressed in a wind jacket and rubber boots)

ALICE   Hi, Davy!

DAVEY   What's up?

ALICE   Upstairs! Covered the little'n wi' shit.

DAVY   Oh! *(He begins to take off his jacket. ALICE studies him)*

ALICE   Where you been?

DAVY   Doon by.

ALICE   On the fish quay?

DAVY   So what?

ALICE   Get yor hammers if she finds out. Better hide them wellies.

(DAVY considers confiding a secret. He stands up holding his boots)

DAVY   Gotta job.

ALICE   Gotta what?

DAVY   Gotta job.

ALICE   On the fish quay?

DAVY   Start o' Monday.

ALICE   Ye haven't?

DAVY   Wanna bet?

ALICE   Eee! what ye ganna tell Ma?

DAVY   *(Doubtful)* Jus' tell her.

ALICE	She'll gan crackers.
DAVY	Who cares?
ALICE	She'll lose hor blob.
DAVY	*(Irritated)* Alreet! Alreet!
ALICE	What aboot yor interview for the Town Clerk's?
DAVY	*(Contemptuous)* Oh! that! That's had it.
ALICE	Eee! She'll gan daft.

(Offstage MA can be heard returning)

MA	Bloody wasters.
ALICE	She's comin'!
MA	Neither work nor want.

(At the sound of his mother, DAVY panics, grabs his jacket and boots and prepares to bolt into the kitchen)

DAVY	Now you shut yor gob, Alice, or A'll shut it for ye.
ALICE	Push off.

(DAVY retreats into the kitchen. ALICE turns up the radio and a second later MA comes in through the main door)

MA   A dunno. He'll put nowt in that bin. 'Cept a Friday when he's passin' it on the way ti the social security. Ye bugs. Likes o' them pickin' up a ticket. Alice! Torn that blarin' thing off. *(MA switches the radio off)* One row after another. *(From the kitchen comes the sound of a tap running. MA looks in the direction of the sound)* Is there somebody out there? Davy? Davy? is that you son? *(She pauses, then shouting)* Davy!

DAVY   Aye, ma!

(DAVY comes in. He pushes past his mother snatches the comic from his sister and sits)

5

MA   Come on bonny lad, it's past five o'clock. *(She sniffs inquiringly in the air)* Yor da wi' ye?

DAVY   No, ma.

MA   S'funny, could've sworn A smelled him.

DAVY   Gotta lock in. Doon at Charlie's.

MA   *(Outraged)* Gotta what? Has he had you in the boozer?

DAVY   Aw. ma! A'm ownly fifteen.

MA   An yor a big fifteen, an' yor da's a big idiot. Now come on, A want the truth.

DAVY   Jus' seen him gannin' in with his mates. Ye knaa! Chopper, Sainty, Danny Mac. Charlie gi' them a lock in.

MA   Mates! Bloody wasters more like it. Dissolvin' thor brains wi' broon ale. Three card brag 'till yon time. They'll take him ti the cleaners. another short week. *(Suspiciously, MA sniffs again. She comes directly over to DAVY and bend over him)* Poo! It's you. It's you, isn't it? Ye smell like a gut barrel. No wonder A thought yor father was in the hoose.

DAVY   Aw, ma.

MA   Ye've been doon on that quay, haven't ye?

DAVY   Ma!

MA   Now come on. A want no lies.

DAVY   Just gi' me da a hand ti wash a few boxes oot. Gettim a quick finish.

MA   A'll finish him.

DAVY   Bob Wilson give's a quid.

MA   Nivvor mind aboot Bob Wilson. Ye'll get the smell o' fish on ye. Gans right thro' yor claes, into yor skin, an' thor's no gettin' rid of it.

6

DAVY   Ma!

MA   Now, Davy, A've telled ye. *(She goes to the mantelpiece to take a letter from an ornament. While her back is turned ALICE gestures to DAVY urging him to tell his MA about the job. DAVY summons up his courage)*

DAVY   Ma! When A was on the quay...

MA   Now look, son, forget about the quay. Ye've got that interview next week. *(She demonstrates the letter)* This is your chance in life. Ye've got yor O-levels. Davy it's yor chance ti mix wi better people.

DAVY   What's better aboot them?

MA   Well, maybe thor no better than us son, but thor not on casual. They've got positions. Davy it's yor place on the bus. Don't end up like yor da.

DAVY   Nowt wrong wi' me da.

MA   Nowt wrong wi' donkeys, but the' divven let them on busses.

DAVY   Sooner hev me da, than any o' them in the Toon Clerk's. All paper hankies for snot rags.

MA   Davy! Divven be si coarse.

DAVY   Ma, hev ye seen them? Stuck in thor desks. No proper winders ti look out. All that frosty glass, like the' hev in bogs. Pathetic! Sittin' pretendin' ti be doin' summick important. All the time, starin' sideways, ti see who's comin, an' gannin', wishin' it was thorselves. Might as well be at skule.

MA   School, Davy. School, not skule.

DAVY   All right! School, skule, what's the difference?

MA   A'll tell ye what the difference is. It's when the' go home at night. Thor not comin' ti the Ridges estate. No, they're livin' where flowers has the chance o' growin', an' a young laddie like you isn't just summick the polis

7

has ti keep an eye on. Where ye can hev respect, an' yor own front door, an nee female welfare supervisor demandin' to be in, ti cut yor pride off at the knees. Aye, by God, that's the dif'rence. *(Pause. She moves across to the window to glance out)* Aye, an' when the' hang thor washin' oot in the mornin', it's still there at dinner time.

DAVY   Ma, yor a patter merchant. Should hev ye on the tele.

MA   Ridges estate! What are wi? Just a joke. Ridges estate! Them that keeps thor coals in the bath. Go to a store for credit. Ridges estate? The' don't want ti know. Go for a decent job. Ridges estate? No chance.

DAVY   How come A got that interview then?

MA   That proves yor somethin' special, Davy. Somebody seen ye were dif'rent. Somebody's took a fancy ti ye.

DAVY   Hold on, ma. Don't want nobody fancyin' us.

MA   Son, it's yor chance in life. Ye don't want a dead end job. Toss away all your education. All that study. Don't let yourself down Davy, an' don't let me down.

DAVY   Ma, yor not on. Things isn't like that now.

MA   Like what?

DAVY   Gettin' a good job in an office. Security, all that jazz. That went out wi' trams. Thor's better money on the docks.

MA   Aye, an' how long will that last? Thor clawin' each other's back now, for a share o' the meat.

DAVY   A can get twenty pound a week startin' money on the quay.

MA   Little apples, Davy. That's yor da talkin', an' it's little apples.

DAVY   An' extras.

MA   What extras?

DAVY   A bit fiddle.

MA   *(Outraged)* Fiddle! What's a laddie like you talkin' about fiddle?

DAVY   Nowt wrong wi' fiddle. Not like pinchin', it's just… fiddle. Da says every job on the quay has ti have a fiddle, or the' cannot keep the men.

MA   Well, it sounds more like Mantovani's bloody orchestra ti me.

DAVY   Aw, ma!

MA   Now look, A'm havin' no argument. You were brought up ti touch nothin' that doesn't belong ye. Yor keepin' away from it. The fish quay is nowt but the home o' the forty thieves, an' A nivvor brought ye into the world ti be a fiddler.

(Offstage, DA can be heard returning. He is a robust, friendly man, only aggressive when frustrated. Heavy with drink, he is singing. His pocket bulges with a bottle of brown ale and with his filleting knife wrapped in a cloth. The sleeves of his jacket are sawn off at the elbows, in the manner of all fish filleters, to keep them from dipping in the trough)

DA *(O.S.)* 'It's not unusual ti be loved by anyone, da dee dee da.'

(The door opens and DA enters. He resonantly belches)

MA   That's lovely! Lovely A must say. Gi yor family the benefit o' yor company.

DA   *(Smiling with the satisfaction of the belch)* That's me. that's yor da. Why give it away ti strangers. *(He advances on MA. Takes hold of her in a clumsy embrace. Forces her to dance. Sings)* 'Stranger in the night, da, da, dee, da, strangers in the night'.

MA   *(Forces herself free)* Gerroff ye great puddin'. *(She goes off into the kitchen. DA takes off his jacket, puts it round the back of his chair and plants his bottle of brown ale on the table)*

DA   Puttin' that kettle on or what?

MA *(O.S.)* A'm puttin' the kettle on.

DA   Worra woman. Hellow Davy! That's my bonny lad. *(Ruffles his son's hair)* All right, son?

DAVY   All right, da.

DA   *(Lowering his voice)* Hey! See them haddocks we were cuttin'. Eh? *(He demonstrates with his hands an approximate eight-inch length)* A says ti Bob Wilson, what di ye call these? he says 'Haddocks'. A says, 'Haddocks, ye mean dog's dicks.' 'm no kiddin' the' were no bigger'n dog's dicks.

            (MA comes back in carrying a teapot, just in time to catch the obscenity of the remark)

MA   Do you hev ti use language like that an' yor own bit lassie sittin' there?

DA   Ooo! listen sanctimonious! Hey! There's a big word eh? Sang titty monious. Hey, ma, yor all right, till you get sang titty monious.

MA   Gawd! *(She moves back into the kitchen. From this point onwards she goes back and forward from living room to kitchen laying the table)*

DA   Hellow, Alice. *(He leans over and cuddles her)* My little lass. *(He goes and looks in the sideboard drawer for a bottle opener)* My little stay-all-day-in-the-house Alice. All right, pet?

MA   She stays in all day, 'cos she's given up fightin' sixty other bairns for a share o' the street.

DA   All right, ma. All right. A'm just sayin' hellow!

MA   Hev ye seen hor leg? Are ye bothered? Twelve stitches in, from the raggy end of a bottle.

DA   A know. A know! Still! She's got ti learn ti stick up for horsel'. *(To ALICE)* You stick up for yorsel', pet.

	Fightin's natural, an' us is a fightin' family. Wi nivvor give up. Nivvor! You show 'em. *(He sits)*
MA	Huh!
DA	A telled ye what General Montgomery sayed to us.
MA	Not that again. *(She disappears into the kitchen)*
DA	*(Rising up)* General Mongomery *(Calling out to MA)* personally ti me. *(To the kids)* S'fact! Standin' as near ti me as your are now. Ganna be this big do on, oot in the desert, y'know. Well, all the top brass was round ti gi' the lads a clap on the back. 'Corporal Rutter, 9268754, Royal Northumberland Fusiliers, sor.' Mongomery says, 'Kerprel', 'Kerprel', 'e says, 'Course he had this funny way o' taalkin', 'cos he's Irish y'know. 'Kerprel,' 'e says, 'You'se Geordies is fighters.' That's what 'e says, 'Fighters'. That was the famous general, Sir Bernadette Montgomery. Give wi all fifty tabs a piece. Couldn't smoke 'em. Bloody horrible. Owld bastard. But 'Fighters', pet, that what 'e sayed. So you show them Alice. Anyhow Ma, where's the rest o' the bairns?
	(MA returns)
MA	One in the pram ootside, ye probably fell ower hor withoot noticin'.
DA	Now, ma, canny on. No rows eh? We want no rows.
MA	What di ye want? A roll call? Yor other three's out roamin' the railway. In the hands o' God, or the neighbours, whichever's the worst.
DA	Well, the bloody railway! They've never mended that fence. Not since the bairns took it down for Guy Fawkes. But look pet, A'm home for a bit o' peace an quiet. So let's have no rows, eh? That grub comin' or what?
MA	*(Vehemently)* It's comin'. *(She leaves. DA pours himself the beer. There is a pause)*
DA	That's my Davy. All right, son. Yor a good'n. Hey, no kiddin', ye did yor da proud this mornin'. *(MA comes in*

to catch the comment) Ooo' sorry. *(Absurd gesture of secrecy)* Nuff sed!

DAVY   S' all right, da. She knows A was on the quay.

MA   Yor encouragin' him to go down there.

DA   Me?

MA   Yes, you.

DA   Not me.

MA   Fine example you are.

DA   Ma, A've told ye. That laddie's got his own mind ti make up. He'll do what he wants ti do, and gan where he wants ti gan.

MA   He's goin' for that interview.

DA   What interview?

MA   Ye know fine well what interview. The Town Clerk's.

DA   The *(Scornfully)* Toon Clerk's.

MA   Yes, the Toon Clerk's an he's goin' for that interview.

DA   Ye've sayed that already.

MA   And I'm sayin' it again. So he knows where he stands *(She goes back into the kitchen making a decisive clatter of crockery)*

DA   *(Calling after her)* Ma, wor Davy's a sunshine lad. Y'know.
'E likes it oot in the fresh air, where the seagulls is flying roond. Huh' thor's no bloody seagulls in the Toon Clerk's.

MA *(O.S)*   'Course thor's not, ye dope. What would the' be wantin' wi seagulls. Dirty, shitty things.

12

DA   *(Taken aback by the vehemence)* That grub comin', or what.

MA *(O.S)*   A've telled ye it's comin'.

DA   So's Chris'mas.

MA   Alice come here, giv's a hand.

     (ALICE goes through to the kitchen to help bring in the plates of food)

DA   *(To DAVY)* Tell ye what. She'll have you in a bowler hat, wi' stripey pants.

DAVY   Not me.

DA   Gi' yor mates a laugh.

DAVEY   Not likely.

DA   Toon Clerk's! Call that work? Ye bugs! Sittin' on thor backsides all day, pushin' a pen. Work! Hey! See what me an big Mutt lifted on the Grimsby wagon, eh? Ten ton! Ten bloody ton! Box, by box. None o' yor fancy fork lifts. Hundredweight, by hundredweight. Aye, an' the rain beatin' on wi. Now, that's what ye call work. Not a writer born, can write that down.

MA *(O.S)*   What ye sayin' to him?

DA   *(Calling back)* Trouble we' you, ma, ye place too much store on education. Yor tryin' ti be upstairs, an' doonstairs at the same time. An' what di ye get? Stuck on the landin'.

     (DAVY and DA enjoy the joke. MA comes in with the food and they all gather at the table. MA plants DA's plateful savagely in front of him)

MA   Just fill yor gob wi' chips, and let's have the biggest relief since Dunkirk. That bairn's goin' ti make use o' his education.

DA   Education!

13

MA   Alice! Davy! Sit down, get yor grub.

DA   A'll tell ye somethin' about education. *(He speaks between mouthfuls of food)* It's no good ti the workin' class. Thor's two kinds of education. The kind the give ti us, and the kind the keep for thorselves. An' the kind the give ti us, yor better off withoot.

MA   What do you know about education?

DA   Don't talk to me about education.

MA   What would be the point?

DA   Listen, what di ye think the idea is? So's we can better worselves? Don't kid on. Listen, the idea of education, is ti make the likes of us, useful ti the buggars that's gettin' the money. Education! Education don't make the job fit you. Education makes you fit the job. Listen, them desks in the Toon Clerk's was there long before he was born.

MA   Jus' gerron wi' yor dinners, take no notice.

DA   Eh? What did ye say? Take no notice… Don't you tell them ti take no notice o' me. *(Everyone stops eating. She has pushed DA too far)* There's a fine… What ye mean, tellin' them that, eh? *(Shouting, half-rising and pointing his finger at MA)* Don't you bloody tell them ti take no notice o' me. what a thing ti say. A'm tellin' them summick important. Don't you tell them ti take no notice o' me.

(There's a stunned silence, DA sits and moodily begins to eat. He looks up at them)

DA   All right! All right! Gerron wi' yor dinners. Education! Puts ye at a desk, or on a machine, an' that's what's wrong wi' this country. Too many machines, an' too many in bloody offices. *(They resume eating. He speaks to his son)* Tell ye what, put me on a machine once. Aye! one o' them fork lift trucks. Hey' laugh. Well A could manage it all right. No bother. Switch it on. Into gear! Giddup! A went off along the factory floor… an' strite thro' the bloody office. *(DAVY and DA and ALICE laugh. MA doesn't think it's funny)* Hey', that fettled them. A says… A says, 'A'm sorry, but A don't think A've quite got the hang of it.' Eeee! ye bugs, laugh! 'Gerris cards.' 'Gerrim out.' But what A'm tryin' to tell ye, son, the laddie that's drivin' that truck now, what's he pickin' up, eh? A mankey thirty-five pound fifty. Why, it's washers. Look, look. A'll show ye. (*DA rises up and fishes into his hip pocket. He brings out a roll of money*) See that. See that handful. Sixty-four quid. Eh? How's that? Casual! In the hand! Sixty-four quid. That's what yor da picked up this week. Wi no education, son, ye might be no good ti nobody but yorsel', but it leaves ye we' no choice but ti get on. (*DA reaches round for his jacket. He removes his filleting knife from the pocket and unrolls the cloth covering it*)

DA   Look, A'll show ye. There ye are. that's all ye need, a good filleting knife. That's the instrument. Carve yousel' a career.

MA   What di ye want, bringing a wicked thing like that here.

DA   That's how ye cut 'em. (*He demonstrates the filleting of a fish*)

MA   Put it away.

DA   A mean it's a simple thing a knife. Eh? But what was ever invented that's more effective?

MA   Will ye put it away.

(*Suddenly and alarmingly DA's temper changes. The kids are frightened. The knife has the appearance of a dagger*)

DA   Will you shut yor silly hole. Shurrup! Shurrup! A'm talkin' ti them. Tryin' ti tell them somethin'. Ye's never listen to us, none o' ye.

DAVY   A really fancy the inshore fishin' da, if A could get...

DA   You as well, shurrup! Never bloody listen. that's another thing about education, gettin' them that's had it to shurrup. (*DAVY gets up from his chair and walks away from his father. DA watches him go and lumbers unsteadily after him*) Now look Davy!... Son! Don't you walk away from me. (*DAVY slumps into the big easy chair*) 'Cos A'm tellin' ye... (*DAVY ignores his father. DA attempts to*

15

rationalise) Look, A sayed there was two kinds of education. Aye, well there's another sort of education, an' it's the sort ye get for yorsel'. Look! Look! *(It's almost as though he would embrace his son)* Bob Wilson! Take Bob Wilson! Y'know Bob. Eh? Comes cryin' ti me. Right? Got fifty boxes on his hands, right? Y'know, cod, haddock, plaice, what have ye. Right? How much Bob? How much? Fifty pence a box? Not on. Not on Bob. Sixty pence a box. Seventy pence a box. Ye want them filleted? Eighty pence a box. He's over a barrel, see? A squeeze the sod. A've got this. *(He bandishes the knife)* Aye, an' A can use it. A'm a skilled man. the' need me. Hev knife, will travel, an' thor's no arguin' wi' the uneducated. *(He goes back to the table and picks up the roll of notes)* Look son, look. Sixty-four quid. Not bad eh? If you can do like yor da, son, we'll be rollin'. *(He throws the roll of notes over the MA. She pushed them away from her)*

MA   Aye, an' where's yor sixty-four quids on the lay off weeks. When thor's no fish comin' in. What about the weeks wi' nowt?

DA   Woman! It's the rough wi' the smooth.

MA   Yor brains is locked behind iron bars. It's not a matter o' money.

(DA furiously sweeps the money and half the table crockery onto the floor)

DA   Ivvorythin's a matter o' money. Ivvorythin's a matter o' money.

(DA leaps to his feet)

DAVY   Don't da. Don't.

MA   Ye great destructive beast. It's a matter o' livin' like people, not animals. Alice, away ootside, an' mind that bairn.

(ALICE scatters out of the room)

DA   What's the matter, is the money not good enough for ye?

MA   No, it's not.

DA   What more di ye want?

DAVY   Don't, man, da. Don't.

DA   Shurrup. What more di ye want?

MA   A'll tell ye what A want. A want the bairns brought up decent, an' not hearin' their mother shoutin' blue murder ti the neighbours every Saturday night.

DA   Gerraway ti hell. Stuffin' their heads wi' that rubbish. An' what difference would it make to us where wi lived? An' di ye think the wives in posh houses don't shout blue murder. Aye, maybes the' do it quieter, 'cos they've been educated ti be polite. An' if the neighbours heard them, they'd be ower polite to listen.

        (During DA's speech MA has begun to pick up the scattered debris from the floor)

DAVY   Da!

DA   Leastways ye've always got that fanny Ann from over the path ti come round slaverin' sympathy. *(Mocking)* 'What's the matter pet, has he been beltin' ye?' 'Is 'e away doon ti Charlie's again.' 'Eee poor soul, what ye have ti put up with.'

DAVY   Da, lay off.

DA   It makes ye bloody sick. *(Thumps the table)* Us is born, an' bred in this Ridges estate, an' thor's no changin' that. An' thor's no changin' us. *(To DAVY)* An' the sooner she gets the daft ideas out of hor head the better. *(Closes up on MA)* Look! Ye want that laddie ti better hisself, eh? that what ye want? Well let him go where the money is.

MA   You, ye pull everythin' down ti your level.

DA   An' you. You! Ye'd turn me own bairns against us.

DAVY   Da, man, leave it be.

DA   Turn me own bairns against us. 'Cos ye haven't the sense ti be content with what ye have.

MA   Be content with what A have!

DA   Yes.

MA   What is it A've got? Go on, tell us.

DA   Ye've got a bloody roof over yor heed for a start.

MA   A've ti be greatful for that? Is it all right livin', an behavin' like pigs, as long as w'are dry pigs?

DA   Yor mother an' father were glad of a roof over thor head.

MA   Aye, me mother an' father come out o' the low street. Yes, they were slum clearance, but the' were happy.

DA   *(With contempt)* Happy!

MA   Yes, happy! That's somethin' thor's no room for here. Like thor's no room for hope, an' no room for love.

DA   Love! *(As though it were a sick word)* Ye great soft bitch. What's that got ti do with it?

DAVY Don't, da.

MA   Aye, A'm a soft bitch. Found that out the night A married you, an' yor mates carried ye upstairs.

DA   A've given ye six bairns.

MA   Yes, mevves yor not fit ti drive a fork lift truck but thor's one job ye proved yorsel' on.

DA   That's right, get yor bloody joke in.

MA   It's no joke. But yor not top o' the league. Upstairs has given his soft bitch nine, next door has got eight, and the soft bitch ower the path has ten up ti now.

DA   What's that got ti do wi' me, ye daft bat?

MA   It's what A'm sayin', yor not responsible. Ye've no more talent that what it takes ti fillet a fish, but yor allowed ti run yor own private orphanage, an' ye've got it that crowded thor queuein' for the netty.

(Infuriated and still wielding the knife, DA lunges at MA)

DA   Ye talk a load o' rubbish.

(DAVY darts across, grabs his father by the arm and hangs on fiercely)

DAVY   Da! Da!

DA   Nowt but a load o' rotten rubbish. All the time, rubbish! Rubbish! *(He tries to break free of DAVY)*

DAVY   Da! A've gotta job! A've gotta job, da.

(DA looks at DAVY uncomprehendingly)

DA   What you talkin' about. Job! Job! What job! *(He calms down)*

DAVY   A've gotta job, da. Bob Wilson set us on.

DA   Eh?

DAVY   Gotta job on the quay wi' Bob Wilson.

MA   Davy, what ye sayin'?

DAVY   A'm sorry, ma.

MA   Davy!

DA   What ye talkin' about, Bob sayed nothin' ti me.

DAVY   Right enough, da. After ye'd gone 'e asked us if A wanted a start.

MA   Ye see. Ye see what ye've done.

DA   A've told ye, woman, A know nothin' about it. *(To DAVY)* Look, A'm yor father. Now A'm entitled to know what's goin' on.

DAVY   He's startin' four school leavers on Monday. He's got three. He asked us if a wanted the job. Twenty pounds a week.

DA   Oh Davy, what ye done?

DAVY   Twenty pounds, ma. It's ownly twelve at the Town Clerk's. It's another eight quid.

(Pause)

DA   Well, A know nothin' about it. Nothin'. *(Pause)* Anyhow, what's Bob wantin' wi' four young laddies?

DAVY   He's puttin' a machine in.

DA   Machine? What machine?

DAVY   A filletin' machine, da.

(There is a pause as DA struggles with the news)

DA   A what?

DAVY   A filletin' machine, da. Bob says ye just feed the fish in, it goes thro' the machine, an' comes out the other end all cut.

DA   A know what a filletin' machine is.

DAVY   There's no experience necessary.

(Pause)

DA   Ye bugs. Nobody tells ye nothin' ti yor face.

DAVY   Bob says thor installin' it this week-end.'E reckons it'll cut fifty stone an hour.

(Pause)

DA   Why is it? Nobody tells ye nothin' ti yor face.

DAVY   Reckons it's fantastic. Even small fish. Just rattles them thro'.

DA   S'what gets me. The' cannot come out with it.

DAVY   Has these nylon gears.

DA   Fifty stone an hour eh?

DAVY   That's what Bob says.

DA   Aye, well that's more'n a filleter's days work.

DAVY   Bob says the blades are…

DA   Oh, ti hell wi' what Bob says.

(Pause)

MA   Davy! Get away out.

DAVY   What's the matter, ma.

MA   Go on, get away out.

DAVY   What've A done? A mean…

MA   Just get away out, Davy. Don't bother your da.

DAVY   *(Disgruntled)* A dunno! What we' always fightin' for?

(He leaves and DA slumps in a chair)

DA   Nivvor ti yor face, that's what gets me. If they'd just come an' tell ye ti yor face.

(MA resumes her tidying up)

MA   Some things the' cannot say to a man's face.

DA   There was talk, like – ye know. Thor's always talk. But nobody ever comes out straight with it.

MA   A'll pour ye out a fresh cup o' tea.

DA   No. Don't bother.

MA   It's no bother. Look it's still hot.

DA   No it's all right. Look... *(Awkward pause)* I'm sorry about the mess.

MA   It's all right. Big seas rock the little boats. *(She pours him out a fresh cup of tea. He is hunched over and she has to go close to him to offer the tea. This is a moment of truth. Despite the abusive row, when the chips are down, MA is the support figure)* Here!

DA   Ta! *(He takes the tea with one hand. With his other hand he reaches her... He does not drink his tea but nurses it in his hands. The door opens and ALICE enters)*

MA   Told you ti stay out an' mind the bairn.

ALICE   Met Danny Mac. Sent us up with a message for da.

DA   Message? What message?

ALICE   'E says, 'Tell yor da from Bob Wilson, not ti bother comin' down on Monday ,'cos thor's nowt expected'.

(Pause. DA looks pathetically at MA. He is shattered)

DA   Ye buggar! Eh! Danny Mac! What's the matter wi' them? Bob tells Danny Mac. Danny Mac he tells her. What's the matter, the' cannot come and tell me ti me face?

MA   Mevves be a bit hard ti tell a man to his face... *(Regretting what she is committed to say)* that he's not wanted.

(DA rouses himself to salvage his pride. He gets up from his chair and grabs his jacket)

DA   What's 'e say? Nowt expected. Is that what 'e says. Aye, well that's what they bloody think.

(He storms out. MA resumes clearing up)

MA   Was the bairn asleep?

ALICE   Yes.

MA   Better off, stayin' with her dreams. Look, help us clear up this mess. All them papers strewed there, pick the up. There's a good lass. Stuff them back on the mantelpiece, the' might be important. *(ALICE complies but then stops to study her school report which she discovers on the mantelpiece)* What ye readin'?

ALICE   Nothin'.

MA   Nothin'?

ALICE   Jus' me school report.

MA   Let's have a look.

ALICE   What for?

MA   Let's have a look. A want ti see it. *(ALICE hands it over)* 'Maths – lacks con-cen-tration. English – some improvement this term. Hist'ry – capable of better.' Music – didn't knaa ye took music.

ALICE   Oh' aye.

MA   'Music – shows considerable, apt– apti–' What's this word?'

ALICE   Aptitude.

MA   Well, that's good, isn't it?

ALICE   'Spose so.

MA   An' you've got it considerable. Well that's nice, Alice. You know it's a good thing ti be good at is music. Mevves ye should take it up. Learn the piana.

ALICE   Yor jokin', ma.

MA   No, A'm not jokin', luv. Music's a luvely thing ti hev. Somethin' A always fancied meself, learnin' the piana.

23

ALICE   Where'd we get a piana?

MA   Thor ownly fifty pence a week. A was thinkin' about doin' a bit part-time again. They'd have us back in the shop anytime. Yes, music, that's a good thing ti have Alice.

ALICE   What would the' say round here if the' heard we had a piana?

MA   The' wouldn't mind that. Folks like a bit o' music. Why yor welcome anywhere if ye can play an instrument. It brings pleasure. Well, it's not just for yorself, this apt–, apti–

ALICE   Aptitude.

MA   Aye. Well that means it's like a gift. Summick ye've got inside ye. Summick that's all yor own. But ye can share it. Ye understand pet. But when ye hev summick inside ye, ye hev ti do somethin' about it. 'Cos it's always like waitin', wantin' ti be brought out into the light.

(ALICE does not believe anything. She switches on her radio and there is music. She picks up her comic and immerses herself in it. MA looks helplessly at her)

The End

Time and Money

This play was originally titled *The Pigeon Man* and was first performed at a Miners' Social Club in Shiremoor, North Tyneside in 1974.

Original Cast

Charlie — Ray Stubbs

Arthur — Tim Healy

Son/Neighbour/Spiv — Sammy Johnson

Directed by Murray Martin

The photo shows Tim Healy as Arthur

CHARACTERS

ARTHUR

Sixty. Fish Curer. Always in dungarees, cloth cap, rubber boots. Hands and face stained with kipper dye.

His life gravitates between his pigeon cree on the top, and the curing sheds at the foot of Tanners Bank, North Shields.

CHARLIE

Arthur's workmate. Sixty-four. Arthritic. Mentally and physically inadequate, but with a degree of slyness.

GERALD

Arthur's son. Thirty. A van salesman with executive pretensions.

NEIGHBOUR

In the allotment. Retired.

FISHWIFE ONE

Young. Neice to Aurthur.

FISHWIFE TWO

Fifty's.

A SILENT THIEF

Middle age.

'STOP OUT STANLEY'

A blue Cheq racing pigeon.

EXT. ALLOTMENTS & PIGEON CREES. TANNERS BANK,
NORTH SHIELDS. BELOW. THE FISH QUAY
& THE CURING SHEDS.

(Outside the sheds two fishwives split herring. At the apron of a cree, the neighbour rattles a can of grain, following the flight of his pigeons. Whistling them down.)

NEIGHBOUR   Coomon! Coomon! Coomon! *(Rattle. Rattle. Rattle)* Coomon!

(ARTHUR emerges from an adjoining cree. Holding a blue check pigeon. The NEIGHBOUR glances over.)

NEIGHBOUR   Combine champion Arthur?

ARTHUR   Got ti be jokin'. Little bloody waster this'n. *(Intimately to the bird)* What are ye? Little bloody waster... Aren't ye? Aye! Ye can nod yor heed.
(To the NEIGHBOUR) Mind his muther was a good'n.

NEIGHBOUR   That's right Arthur. She was!

ARTHUR   *(To the bird)* Oh aye! Yor muther was good ti me. And yor ganny! She was a good'n. By God she was. A good'n! But you, ye little ... flamer... what ye like?

NEIGHBOUR   No way you can work it out Arthur. Coomon! Coomon! *(Rattle. Rattle. Rattle)* A doubt he's a throwback. Coomon!

ARTHUR   Bloody throw out more like. *(Intimately to the bird)* Haven't gorrit upstairs have ye? Eh! Have ye? Cannit get yorsel' sorted. What's the matter with ye, eh? *(Affectionately strokes the bird)*

NEIGHBOUR   What's your Gerald think?

ARTHUR   (*To the bird*) Oh Gerald! What's he say. The chop! That's what he says doesn't 'e? Chop! Chop!....

NEIGHBOUR   No good being soft Arthur. Pigeon racin' and sentiment don't mix. Coomon! Coomon! (*Rattle. Rattle*)

ARTHUR   Right!

NEIGHBOUR   So! Ye puttin' him in?

ARTHUR   See when Gerald comes.

                (*Offstage. The sudden, then incessant barking of a dog*)

                Oo! Talk o' the devil.

                (*GERALD appears at a distance. At the allotment gate. His progress impeded by the dog*)

GERALD   Go on! Gerroff ye twat!

                (*The dog increases its aggression.*)

ARTHUR   Just come through the gate Gerald.

GERALD   Yor jokin'. No way. Gerroff ye black bastard.

ARTHUR   Be alright!

GERALD   It's bloody ridiculous. I'm tellin' ye da! This is it. The finish. Go on! Piss off! ...

ARTHUR   It's on a rope.

GERALD   On a rope! On friggin' crack! Get back! Ye sod ... How man! Da! Fer Cris' sake, call the bastard off ...

ARTHUR   Come off ye bastard. Come off ...

(The dog subsides. GERALD comes through the gate)

GERALD   Gerroff!

GERALD   *(Closes)* Bloody ridiculous! ...

ARTHUR   Well, y'know son. It's your own makin'. Ye gorron kickin' it. I told ye! Kickin'... kickin'... It's took a dislike ti ye ...

NEIGHBOUR   Coomon! Coomon! *(Rattle. Rattle. Rattle)*

GERALD   What ye got there?

ARTHUR   Eh?

GERALD   *(Investigating the Blue Cheq)* Aw! not Stop Out Stanley. Fer Cris' sake.

ARTHUR   Y'see son... A thought mebbe ...

GERALD   Y'not puttin' him in...

ARTHUR   This race could sort'm out.

GERALD   Sort'm out? Take a half brick! Da man, they're gettin' uppined.

NEIGHBOUR   Right Arthur! They're gettin' uppined.

GERALD   Gettin' uppined alright. It's five hundred mile ti France.

NEIGHBOUR   Better pack'm a life jacket Arthur.

ARTHUR   What y'reckon then son?

GERALD   Da. He's an eatin' an' shittin' machine full stop.

ARTHUR   Yor right son.

GERALD   An' he's daft

(ARTHUR cups his hand over the pigeon's head to shield it from the abuse)

ARTHUR   True.

GERALD   Snap its bastard head off.

ARTHUR   Y'reckon?

GERALD   Da! Man! We don't keep'm for ornaments.

ARTHUR   *(To NEIGHBOUR)* He's right.

              (To GERALD) Yor right son.

GERALD   Time an' money da! He gans in circles.

NEIGHBOUR   Coomon! Coomon! *(Rattle. Rattle.)*

GERALD   Have ye gorrim boxed?

ARTHUR   If ye hang on.

GERALD   Not bloody hangin' on da. Not goin' through that gate wi' me hands tied. Look! fetchim down ti the smokehouse.

ARTHUR   Oh! right son. A will!

GERALD   A'll get them up ti the transporter, an' see ti the register.

ARTHUR   You're a good'n son. A good'n.
              (To NEIGHBOUR) He's a good'n eh?

NEIGHBOUR   Nice when the' take an int'rest.

GERALD   But mind. A tell ye' Not that'n.

ARTHUR   Give'm the chop eh?

GERALD   A'll give it ye straight da! Knock'm! Pull his fuckin' heed off. Or you an' me is washed... A'm not wastin' me time...

(He leaves Passing through the gate. Offstage the dog growls)

GERALD   You an' all ... piss off! *(Exit)*

ARTHUR   Heart's in the right place.

NEIGHBOUR   He's keen. Ye can see that.

ARTHUR   Oh he's keen alright. Just the dog. The' divven gerron!

NEIGHBOUR   Need a dog Arthur. On these allotments.

ARTHUR   Kick'n. Kick'n. He got me on kick'n. It's watchin' all the time for 'm comin'.

NEIGHBOUR.   It would do... Coomon! Coomon! *(Rattle. Rattle)*

ARTHUR   Well. Better get down see what Charlie's up to.

NEIGHBOUR   Is that owld bugger still wi' ye Arthur?

ARTHUR   Oh! aye!

NEIGHBOUR   Still workin'?

ARTHUR   Work! Doesn't know the meaning o' the word.

(CHARLIE comes out the curing shed to lazily sweep the frontage. The two FISHWIVES observe him while they carry on cutting)

ARTHUR   *(To the pigeon)* Aye yor muther was a good'n. *(He exits back into the cree)*

NEIGHBOUR   Coomon! Coomon! *(Rattle. Rattle. Rattle)* *(Exits)*

• • • •

EXT. THE CURING SHED

(CHARLIE idly sweeping)

OLDER FISHWIFE	Divven strain yorsel' Charlie!
CHARLIE	Seen owt o' Arthur?
YOUNG FISHWIFE	Up bank.
CHARLIE	Oh! Ye gorra tab on ye?
OLDER FISHWIFE	No!
CHARLIE	Eh!
OLDER FISHWIFE	A said, No!
YOUNG FISHWIFE	Somebody want him?
CHARLIE	Who?
YOUNG FISHWIFE	Me Uncle Arthur. Does somebody want him?
CHARLIE	No! Just the boss was on. Ye not ganna give's a tab
OLDER FISHWIFE	Told ye Charlie. Gettin' no more.
CHARLIE	Howway!
FISHWIFE	Ye sweepin' this shit?
CHARLIE	What shit?
OLDER FISHWIFE	This shit.

(CHARLIE studies the offal below their feet)

CHARLIE	That's herrin' shit.
OLDER FISHWIFE	So what?

CHARLIE	*(Indicating his own area)* This is haddock shit.
OLDER FISHWIFE	All shit.
CHARLIE	Naw! Herrin' shit's yor shit. Wor shit's haddock shit.
OLDER FISHWIFE	Charlie!
CHARLIE	Not sweepin' yor shit.....
OLDER FISHWIFE	Charlie!
CHARLIE	Ye think I'm daft.
OLDER FISHWIFE	Charlie!
CHARLIE	I'm not that daft.
OLDER FISHWIFE	Come here. *(CHARLIE approaches with some caution. FISHWIFE indicates her top breast pocket)* Just the one. *(CHARLIE takes out the pack of cigarettes from the pocket. The FISHWIFE keeps her wet hands clear. He puts the cigarette into his own top pocket)*
CHARLIE	Keep it for after.
OLDER FISHWIFE	*(Indicating the pack)* Uh uh! *(CHARLIE replaces the pack into her breast pocket. ARTHUR appears with a pigeon basket supported on the handlebars of a bicycle. CHARLIE spots him and makes a hurried departure)*
OLDER FISHWIFE	What about the shit?
CHARLIE	After... *(Exits)*

OLDER FISHWIFE   (*ARTHUR passing them*) There's the one
                        that's daft.

                        (*ARTHUR exits after CHARLIE*)

                        • • • •

INT. THE SMOKEHOUSE.

                        (*Blackened with a century of smoke.
                        Troughs of orange coloured dye. Empty
                        spits on framing. Baskets. Boxes. Bins.
                        Bags of sawdust shavings. Boxes of fish
                        fillets. Box of whole haddocks. Machine for
                        skinning fillets. Benches. Filleting trough.
                        Benches. Coke stove. Telephone on wall. The
                        one link with the 'boss'.
                        At the far end of the room the entrance to
                        the kiln. The area is bleak. Run down,
                        chaotic. Decaying.
                        On the coke stove a pail of water is kept hot
                        to dip their hands in for relief from the cold.
                        CHARLIE panicking. Throws out the dregs
                        of a cup of tea. Folds up his 'Sun' news-
                        paper, stuffs it into his jacket. Hastily
                        swallows a half eaten bacon sandwich.
                        Removes a fish box that has been serving as
                        a seat by the stove. Puts ARTHUR's bacon
                        sandwich on the stove. Then with a great
                        show of industry moves boxes of fillets from
                        the ground to bench level.
                        ARTHUR enters. A glance at CHARLIE.
                        Not fooled by the activity.
                        ARTHUR places the basket of pigeons onto
                        a bench.
                        CHARLIE comes over to inspect*)

CHARLIE   Got them then?

ARTHUR   What's it look like?

CHARLIE   Gerald be comin' for them is 'e? Hey:
                        Pigee! Pigee! Pigee! Big race eh! France
                        eh! Gettin' uppined. Hey Pigee! Pigee!.

ARTHUR	Hoo! Talk ti pigeons, talk quiet.
CHARLIE	*(Softly)* Pigee! Pigee! Pigee!
ARTHUR	Aw man! Leave 'm be. Get yor great face outa that basket.
	(CHARLIE retreats)
	Frighten them to death. *(ARTHUR surveys the fish boxes)* What's this lot then?
CHARLIE	The fish.
ARTHUR	A can see that. Much have the' sent?
CHARLIE	He didn't say.
ARTHUR	Didn't say? Wouldn't drop a load off an' not say.
CHARLIE	Was all piled on the deck.
ARTHUR	What if it's a stone short? Did ye count 'm? *(Realising the truth)* Ye went out didn't ye?
CHARLIE	No!
ARTHUR	*(Angry)* I told ye ti stay put. Am I talkin' ti mesel' or what?
CHARLIE	Just two minutes ti the Mission cafe for the bacon buns Arthur.
ARTHUR	Let's have a look. *(Inspects the fish)*
CHARLIE	I told the wife ti dip the bread, 'Cos A know that's the way we like them. *(Moves aside to lift more boxes onto bench)* Ye bugga if ye don't ask they'll not do it.
ARTHUR	Looka this. *(Lifting out a small fillet)* Codlin'. Small codlin' The bloody lot. Who do the' think's ganna skin this lot?

CHARLIE	Dunno Arthur.
ARTHUR	A've haddocks to split as well.
CHARLIE	Hopeless.
ARTHUR	Looka the size of them.
CHARLIE	Bloody disgustin'.
ARTHUR	Who do the' think I am... Spider Man!
CHARLIE	Should tell 'm...
ARTHUR	Tell 'm! Oh A'll tell 'm alright. Bloody sure A'll tell 'm... (*ARTHUR moves to mix the dye*) Tell 'm a few more things besides. By God A will.
CHARLIE	Shoulda make ye a cup o' tea Arthur?
ARTHUR	Never mind about bloody tea man. Get them boxes opened up.
	(*CHARLIE searches. ARTHUR watches despairingly. CHARLIE turns to ARTHUR*)
CHARLIE	Seen me knife?
	(*ARTHUR points it out*)
CHARLIE	Ee! Must be gannin' blind. Want it stacked by the machine?
ARTHUR	Naw! On top o' Grey's Monument. Everyday! Everyday, the same daft questions. Does nowt ever click in yor heed. For Cris' sake... Gerron man!
CHARLIE	A put yor bun on the stove Arthur, 'cos when the' go cold the grease gets horrible. (*Thinks*) Grey's Monument! Heh, heh! Grey's Monument!

(ARTHUR stirs the trough of dye... CHARLIE makes a great labour of moving the fillets to the machine. Glances over)

CHARLIE	Doin' the mix?
ARTHUR	What's it look like?
CHARLIE	Is it two or three measures ye put in?
ARTHUR	You leave the mix ti me. By rights A shouldn't have all this ti do.

(CHARLIE returns to sawing off the string binding on the remaining boxes)

CHARLIE	Boss come on!
ARTHUR	Y'what?
CHARLIE	When ye was out. He come on!
ARTHUR	Huh! *(Waits for an answer that is not forthcoming)* Well?
CHARLIE	Eh?
ARTHUR	Well, what did 'e say?
CHARLIE	The boss? Oh 'e said nowt.
ARTHUR	Wouldn't just say nowt.
CHARLIE	Just said, "Where's Arthur?"
ARTHUR	What did you say:
CHARLIE	Oh! A said nowt.
ARTHUR	What di ye mean? Ye said nowt!
CHARLIE	Just said, ye wasn't in.
ARTHUR	Could've said A was fetchin' salt.

(CHARLIE thinks about that)

CHARLIE   But we've got salt Arthur.

ARTHUR   He doesn't know that. Ye daft bat. Not that it bothers me. A'm not bothered. *(ARTHUR goes for a bag of salt (1 cwt) & labours it into position)* Bloody sure! *(ARTHUR lifts the sack up to the trough)*

CHARLIE   Ye want ti watch yor back Arthur.

(ARTHUR heaves the sack over)

ARTHUR   How the friggin' hell can A watch me back man!

CHARLIE   Would've give ye a lift.

ARTHUR   Would've! Aye, would've! Bloody up now.

CHARLIE   Should've asked.

ARTHUR   Shoulda? Ever think o' doing owt without bein' asked? That's another thing. A could do with some proper help round here

(Stirs the salt. Then pushing past CHARLIE moves to the skinning machine. Gestures irritably to the wall 'phone)

ARTHUR   Alright for him. Savin' bloody wages. *(Switches on the machine. Begins to feed the fillets through)* Gawd! Looka this. Bloody blade on this. Never been serviced since it was put in. Be a stack o' waste.

CHARLIE   Ye've telled them about that blade Arthur.

ARTHUR   Boss wants to get hissel round here.

CHARLIE   Couldn't say they haven't been telled.

ARTHUR	Guttin' Skinnin' Packin' Hangin'... Like a bloody horse. Might as well hang me nob out. *(Noticing CHARLIE. Struggling to cut the box bindings)* Is that blunt? Can ye not cut string now?

Rub it up! Rub it up! Here give is it... *(ARTHUR skillfully puts an edge on the knife. Rubbing its edge against a steel. Then slashing open the bindings)*

Fer Cris' sake man! Go an' put the shavin's in the kiln.

(CHARLIE pleased at the prospect. Dips his arthritic hands into the bucket of hot water) |
| CHARLIE | Righto Arthur. Shoulda fire it up? |
| ARTHUR | What the hell's the good o' firin', wi' no fish in the chimney. Just put the shavin's down.

(CHARLIE disappears into the kiln with a bag of shavings) |
| ARTHUR | An' don't spill them all over the place like the last time. |
| CHARLIE *(O.S)* | A'll sweep up for ye Arthur. Before A go. |
| ARTHUR | What? At one o'clock. Think I'll be done by then? Mus' be jokin'. It's not me on part time. What a firm. 'The more ye work, the more ye may, makes no difference ti the pay'

(Pause. In the depth of the kiln CHARLIE is thinking about that) |
| CHARLIE *(O.S)* | *(Out of the depths)* A don't think ye get the money ye should Arthur. |

41

ARTHUR   (*Astonished*) Eh?

CHARLIE (*O.S*)   Not for the hours ye put in.

ARTHUR   Come here!

                        (*No response*)

                        Come here!

                        (*CHARLIE puts his head timidly round the kiln door*)

ARTHUR   How di you know what money A get?

CHARLIE   Oh! eh! A just happened ti see yor envelope.

ARTHUR   Just happened ti see me envelope!

CHARLIE   Well, ye'd left it on the bench.

ARTHUR   You nosey bugga.

CHARLIE   A wasn't lookin' Arthur.

ARTHUR   Ye must've been.

CHARLIE   Naw! Honest Arthur. It was just like lyin' there.

ARTHUR   Well, that's it. That is bloody it. What a place. A'm gettin' things straight here. A'm gettin' it all sorted. My God, let me tell you… when…

                        (*The 'phone rings to cut through the situation. ARTHUR grabs it*)

ARTHUR   (*Angrily*) Hello! (*Subdued*) Oh hello boss! Oh not so bad… Managin' like. Mind, the stuff's a bit small. Aye! bit on the small side. A see… more economic… A see… Well you know the business best boss… yes!

(CHARLIE closes to ARTHUR. Intervening. Tugging at his arm. Pointing to the machine)

CHARLIE

(Forming the words with his mouth) The blade! Tell 'm about the blade!

ARTHUR

(Trying to shrug CHARLIE off) Yes boss! Right boss. Oh! about that blade boss! y'know... on the skinnin' machine...

(CHARLIE picks up the sweeping brush)

CHARLIE

An' this brush as well! Tell 'm it's fucked!

ARTHUR

The skinnin' machine! Oh! a see!... Out of guarantee... Well after ten years, it would be ... Yes... not worth it... No! Well, y'know me boss! A'll not be beat. Sure!... Just A was worried about the waste, wi' the machine being dicky. Eh? Skin it by hand? No! No bother, but it's ten ounce fillets boss. Y'know! Twenty boxes! Fifty fillets ti the box. No! A'm not goin' anywhere! Sure! Right! A'll see it gets a good cure. Want it packed early! Right! Well I could get down sharp in the mornin'... Cool it off first. Aye! right boss!... Yes... Leave it ti me boss. Nowt's a bother... No! Right!... So long boss!

(ARTHUR rings off. Returns to the skinning machine. Looks disconsolately at the pile of fish. He is feeling utterly defeated)

CHARLIE

Shoulda make ye that cup o' tea now Arthur?

• • • •

EXT. THE SHEDS.

(The two FISHWIVES are sitting outside on fish boxes having their break. Tea, tabs, and a sandwich)

43

OLDER FISHWIFE	Always been that sort o' family. Like ye wouldn't know the' were there.
YOUNG FISHWIFE	Anonymous.
OLDER FISHWIFE	Aye! Heeds doon, arses up. *(Unwrapping a sandwich. Handing one to the YOUNGER FISHWIFE)* Tuna! A like Tuna! Mind, yor Uncle Arthur was a craftsman. A'll say that. Still is. Given the chance. Can do the London cure. Y'know, smoked salmon... anythin'. Properly trained is Arthur. Where it all started y'know... London. The Jews that come from Russia, they brought smoke curin'. Not many knows that. Up here was all salt curin'. Anyhow, it's dip, an dye now. Oak chips! That's all gone... Fly curin'. Whip'm in, whip'm out.

(CHARLIE emerges from his shed. Blinks in the light. Leans on his brush)

OLDER FISHWIFE	*(Indicates the need to sweep)* Hey you. Don't forget this.
CHARLIE	After...
YOUNGER FISHWIFE	Dirty job for a woman
OLDER FISHWIFE	Many be glad of it...
YOUNGER FISHWIFE	Not me...
OLDER FISHWIFE	It's money isn't it? We started on ten bob a week.
YOUNGER FISHWIFE	And as many broken kippers... I know...
OLDER FISHWIFE	Aye! Ye think it's funny, but all that sorta thing is comin' back. You young'ens will only believe it when it happens ti you.
YOUNGER FISHWIFE	*(Mimicking)* Ee! 'We used ti feed our babies in the sawdust shed'.

OLDER FISHWIFE	That's true, that is. Yor Uncle Arthur was kept in there, in his pram.
YOUNGER FISHWIFE	In the sawdust shed?
OLDER FISHWIFE	That's right! Yor gran' said, he was no bigger than a milk bottle.
YOUNGER FISHWIFE	Was 'e born in the sawdust shed?
OLDER FISHWIFE	Not sayin' that! Not exactly born in the sawdust shed. But he might've got started off there.
YOUNGER FISHWIFE	How do you mean?
OLDER FISHWIFE	I mean, funny things went on... in the sawdust shed.
YOUNGER FISHWIFE	Eee!
OLDER FISHWIFE	Boss wasn't just a 'phone on the wall them days.
YOUNGER FISHWIFE	Poor Uncle Arthur.
OLDER FISHWIFE	One day yor granny was feedin' him when owld Woodger come in. "Hey!" 'e says, "There'll be no tit in my time." "Not you gettin' it" she says... Vulgar owld bugga he was... Mind he still stood watchin'.
YOUNGER FISHWIFE	Ye mean the boss, an' me gran' ?
OLDER FISHWIFE	There was talk. Know what some are like. Hoo Charlie! You mind them days eh! The little Shields herrin'. *(Sings)* 'Where have all the kippers gone... Two faced bastards everyone' Naw! Yor Uncle Arthur's alright. If right was right. He'd be the boss here tiday. But he's no confidence. First day at school. Shit his pants. Mind don't tell that to nobody. Hey Charlie! How long

45

since the East coast herrin' ban? Ten years? The little silver darlin's. They'll come back. But the men will be gone. Just your Uncle Arthur. Brought up in the sawdust shed, and still here. I doubt he's stuck...

ARTHUR *(O.S)*   Charleeeeeee!

(CHARLIE exits back into the shed)

• • • •

INT. THE SMOKEHOUSE.

(ARTHUR is out of sight, in the chimney of the kiln. He has been hanging spits, and the ladder has slipped. CHARLIE comes to the foot of the kiln, and peers up)

CHARLIE   Alright Arthur?

ARTHUR *(V.O)*   Grab the ladder.

CHARLIE   Y'what?

ARTHUR *(V.O)*   The sodden ladder man! Grab it.

CHARLIE   Just a minute....

ARTHUR *(V.O)*   Fer Cris' sake.

CHARLIE   Just move this spit...

ARTHUR *(V.O)*   Hurry up man! A'm on one leg...

CHARLIE   Righto!

ARTHUR *(V.O)*   I'm bloody goin' man!...

(CHARLIE struggles to manoeuvre the ladder)

CHARLIE   Hang on! Got stuck. Oops! That's it. Y'rup there?

ARTHUR *(V.O)*	Not for fuckin' long…
CHARLIE	Hold on! Hold on! There y'are.

(CHARLIE uprights the ladder, and ARTHUR climbs down emerging from the kiln. Quite shaken…)

ARTHUR	Could've gone there! Y'realise? Coulda come down thirty feet.
CHARLIE	Ye want ti watch it Arthur.
ARTHUR	You shoulda been there. You shoulda been at the foot o' that ladder.
CHARLIE	A was just.…
ARTHUR	A could be bloody mutton. Could be dead…
CHARLIE	Sorry Arthur.

(ARTHUR moves angrily away to resume hand skinning fillets)

CHARLIE	Be the top level filled then is it?
ARTHUR	Just put some spits on the bloody frame.
CHARLIE	Right Arthur…
ARTHUR	Bloody state o' things…

(CHARLIE begins hanging the spits on the frames. ARTHUR goes to the stove to dip his hands into the bucket of warm water. Trying to control his rage. CHARLIE tries another tack)

CHARLIE	Never got your bacon bun Arthur.

(ARTHUR looks down at the bun. Unable to think of a response. Bites it. Feels like spitting it out. Swallows)

47

CHARLIE	Gone a bit dry has it?

(ARTHUR continues to savagely consume the sandwich. It feels like a relief to his feelings)

CHARLIE   Just put these in the kiln.

(CHARLIE wheels the mobile frame into the kiln. Takes his time, observes ARTHUR move across to the bench, and inspect his pigeons. There is a half door to the kiln so CHARLIE can be out of sight off centre)

CHARLIE   It's always amazed me.

ARTHUR   What ye on about?

(Returns to skinning the fillets. Working furiously)

CHARLIE   How the' manage.

ARTHUR   *(With his back to CHARLIE)* How what manages?

CHARLIE   Pigeons!

ARTHUR   Are ye gettin' that frame in? What about pigeons?

CHARLIE   How the' manage.

ARTHUR   Manage what for Cris' sake?

CHARLIE   Gettin' back from France.

ARTHUR   *(Half turning but unable to see CHARLIE)* Look man! Get stuck in. This stuff's ready. *(But he is hooked to a favourite topic)* It's the rays.

CHARLIE   Y'what?

ARTHUR	The rays man! The rays! The' pick up the rays.
	(CHARLIE lights up his tab, with a brand from the fire and nonchalantly leans against the kiln door)
CHARLIE	Who?
ARTHUR	The bloody pigeons man! These invisible rays, the' pick 'm up…
CHARLIE	What sorta rays Arthur?
ARTHUR	Told ye? They're invisible! Nobody properly knows.
CHARLIE	Oh!
ARTHUR	But scientists has proved it.
CHARLIE	Oh!
	(He carefully blows his cigarette smoke into the kiln mingling it with the smoke of the wood shavings. He is not really interested. He has heard it all before. It is a matter of playing ARTHUR along)
ARTHUR	Like the wireless! Either y'know it or ye don't…
CHARLIE	Marvellous that!
	(ARTHUR is not without suspicion. Tries to see)
ARTHUR	Hey! Are you comin' outa that bloody kiln or what?
	(CHARLIE nips his cigarette, pockets the dump, and saunters out)
ARTHUR	Here get this lot hung.

(CHARLIE begins to drape fillets across the second frame of spits. He and ARTHUR are now working side by side)

CHARLIE   How di the' pick the rays up then Arthur?

ARTHUR   With thor brains of course, ye daft bat.

CHARLIE   Oh!

ARTHUR   Whoosh! On their way. No messin'

CHARLIE   Clever that. *(Pause)* What about the ones wi' no brains?

ARTHUR   You bugga! You should know! Go round in circles...Tryin' ti pick the rays up.

CHARLIE   Could follow the ones what's picked up the rays.

ARTHUR   Oh! aye! Could do that. Crafty buggas. But it's a race man! Talkin' about thousands o' birds gettin' tossed into the sky. It's a great mix up.

(Charlie thinks about that. The story is moving into areas he hasn't previously considered)

CHARLIE   Some gets lost then? Don't the'?

ARTHUR   'Course the' do. Get lost!

CHARLIE   What happens to them?

ARTHUR   Who knows? Could just drop in the sea...

CHARLIE   Get drooned?

ARTHUR   Well, the' haven't got bloody webbed feet.

CHARLIE   No!

                           *(ARTHUR pushes some fillets over to
                           CHARLIE to move the job on)]*

ARTHUR   Come on! Come on!
                           Some just wanders off.

                           *(CHARLIE. Struggling. Fumbling the fish
                           with his arthritic hands)*

                           Oh!

ARTHUR   Look, if yor hands is cowld, dip'm in the
                           bucket.

                           *(CHARLIE gladly does this. ARTHUR
                           drapes the fillets, taking over CHARLIE's
                           relinquished role)*

CHARLIE   Where'd the' wander off...?

ARTHUR   Any f...n where! Man! Parks! Bus sta-
                           tions! Cadgin' crumbs! Street peckin'...

CHARLIE   Serves 'm right eh?

ARTHUR   What for?

CHARLIE   Havin' no brains.

                           (ARTHUR lost for words. Recovers)

ARTHUR   Take that bucket, an' give them spits a
                           scrub down.

                           *(CHARLIE looks for the scrubbing brush.
                           Taking the bucket with him. It is a kind of
                           aimless meandering. ARTHUR shakes his
                           head in disbelief)*

CHARLIE   The' must get sick. Do the' not get sick?
                           Sometimes things seem to have no sense.
                           Have ye seen the scrubber? Oh there it
                           is.

                           51

ARTHUR   Ever wonder what you're doin'?

CHARLIE   How do you mean?

ARTHUR   What you're doin' Why yor here!

CHARLIE   Dunno!

ARTHUR   Y' dunno! Have ye not got an objective?

CHARLIE   What's that?

ARTHUR   An objective! Y' dunno what that is! God man! Y' know nowt. Look, d'ye want ti keep yor job here?

CHARLIE   What y' askin' that for Arthur?

                (The debate has taken a threatening turn, and ARTHUR is feeling pleased and dominant. Puts on the pressure)

ARTHUR   'Cos it's a simple question.

CHARLIE   Nobody has said anythin' about packin' in.

ARTHUR   Not sayin' about packin' in. Sayin' do ye want ti keep yor job.

CHARLIE   Aye!

ARTHUR   Well then, that's an objective. Here! Grab on... *(indicates the box of haddocks. One at each end of the box they swing it up onto the bench. Somehow ARTHUR's action is ahead of CHARLIE's, so he is taking the brunt. CHARLIE goes to resume scrubbing the spits)*

ARTHUR   No. Pack in doin' that, an' get those haddocks into the brine.

                (CHARLIE begins to transfer the fish one by one into the trough)

ARTHUR	Look! Ye like a run into the boozer Saturday night. Am I right?
CHARLIE	Don't drink a lot Arthur, y' know that.
ARTHUR	C'mon. Don't kid me. Ye like a pint. eh! Now c'mon Charlie.
CHARLIE	Never go in 'til after ten.
ARTHUR	Still ye like it. the odd pint! And yor tabs. Ye like yor tabs. It's all objectives man!. Oh! for God's sake, not one by one. Tip the bloody lot man! *(He leans over, and heaves the box upside down into the trough. The haddocks tumble in. ARTHUR resumes skinning the small fillets. CHARLIE blows on, and nurses his frozen hands)*
ARTHUR	*(Enjoying CHARLIE's discomfort)* What I'm sayin'. There's always somethin' at the end of the line for pigeons. They've got a good loft, good grub. It's where they get their nookies. Send them off, and all they're thinkin' about is gettin' back. Sharp! An objective! *(Indicating the haddocks)* Stir them round. Get the' muck off. Go on! Stir'em. That's it. Go on! Go on!. Stop! Look can you cut the' heeds off?
CHARLIE	Eh!
ARTHUR	Where's yor knife. Give it a go. Go on!
	(CHARLIE tries to clumsily saw off a haddock head)
	Round the collar! Leave the nape! Break it. Cut, an' break. Go on! Give it a go. Cut an' break! That's it. Go on!... Push the knife in...
CHARLIE	Never done the haddocks before...
ARTHUR	Never too late ti learn. A'll show anybody that's willin'. Go on! Cut, an'

53

break. The collar, the collar, Get behind the collar. Now cut. Go on.

(The head comes away. Charlie *triumphant)*

ARTHUR   There y' are. Now grab anuther. Go on.

CHARLIE   Could get thor grub, an' nookies in France!

ARTHUR   Well that's where yor wrong. Neither man nor beast is livin' in the Garden of Eden no more. What it doesn't do... is grow on trees... O.K!

(Gaining confidence. CHARLIE nods his head in agreement. Vehemently, attacks another haddock head)

CHARLIE   Right!

ARTHUR   Look. What happens when wi finish this box of haddocks.

(CHARLIE puzzles)

CHARLIE   Start anuther one.

ARTHUR   Exactly!

(CHARLIE pleased he has got the answer right)

Today! Tomorrow, the next day! Struggle on! Sometimes the wind's in yor face, sometimes it's at yor back. Ye can expect nowt more than that.

(CHARLIE considers. A cloud darkens his thoughts)

CHARLIE   What if ye have a pigeon... y'know. Cannot pick the rays up?

ARTHUR   Somebody's got ti make a decision. Sort it out. Maybe give it a chance over the distance. *(Pointing his knife at CHARLIE)* But ye cannit carry passengers. Yor standin' ti loss big money. The clock's tickin' on.

(CHARLIE is nodding his head. Agreeing)

Well! What would you do. If it was your bird?

(CHARLIE furiously saws through the haddock's nape, and decapitates the head into a bin)

CHARLIE   Cut its fuckin' heed off!.

(ARTHUR is astonished at the venom. Looks to his pigeon basket. Reminded of his duty)

• • • •

EXT. THE SHEDS.

(The two FISHWIVES sweep up. The elder with the brush, the younger collects the sweepings onto a shovel and transfers the debris into a bin)

YOUNGER FISHWIFE   Might know who'd end up doin' it. Friggin' men!

OLDER FISHWIFE   Nowt changes.

YOUNGER FISHWIFE   Why are we always sweepin' up for them?

OLDER FISHWIFE   If wimmin got paid for bein' daft, I'd be covered in jewellery. Here! Hold that shovel straight... My mother always said, 'keep away from the fish quay, you might fall in.' Wish I'd listened....

(The debris is picked up and put into the bin)

YOUNGER FISHWIFE   That it then?

OLDER FISHWIFE	'Til the next lot. Puttin' the kettle on?
YOUNGER FISHWIFE	Why not…

(They divest their rubber aprons)

(The silent thief appears, sauntering up and down, as though looking for someone. Staring into the distance. Nonchalantly lighting up a cigarette. Pretending to be unaware of the women, keeping a distance from them, being embarrassingly furtive)

YOUNGER FISHWIFE	Men, they're always tryin' to put one over on you.
OLDER FISH WIFE	It's their nature.
YOUNGER FISHWIFE	Can't understand them…
OLDER FISHWIFE	'Cos you listen to them. You want to understand men, never listen to them talkin'. Just watch the way they go on.

(The younger woman becomes aware of the silent thief. She nudges her companion to awareness. The two women stare uncompromisingly at the silent thief, who effects indifference, and keeps up an exaggerated pretence of being at ease)

OLDER FISHWIFE	Tells ye everythin'… Was readin' about it. Called body language.

(The silent thief saunters past them)

Well, maybe wimmin never get wise 'til the' get owld, but men, ye bugga, the longer the' live the dafter the' get… Howway, get in, get that kettle on.

(The silent thief, keeping his face averted until the two FISHWIVES have exited into their shed. Jerks into action. Glances up and down, stubs out his cigarette, and scuttles

into the smokehouse. As he disappears the two women reappear at the door)

OLDER FISHWIFE

The coast must've cleared. See what A mean! Must think we're as daft as their-sel's... No pet! Ye mix wi' men, ye get used. Best keep out o' the way, an' let them get on usin' theirsel's...

(Exit)

• • • •

INT. SMOKEHOUSE.

(CHARLIE sits in the kiln for warmth, eating his sandwiches. Smoking a cigarette. ARTHUR sits by the stove on an upturned box, nursing a mug of tea.
The silent thief enters. He has the shadowy caution of a man whose presence requires no explanation.
ARTHUR jumps to his feet, goes to the door. Looks right and left checking the coast is clear... Returns.
ARTHUR uncovers a parcel of fish hidden under a bench. CHARLIE raises himself to eavesdrop the deal.
An exchange takes place. A few pounds for the fish. No words are spoken. The silent thief conceals the parcel under his jacket. Begins to leave.
ARTHUR pulls him back at the exit. Glancing out to reassure himself the coast is still clear. Waves the silent thief out. The silent thief scuttles up the road. Exit.
ARTHUR returns. Pockets the cash.
CHARLIE drops his gaze. ARTHUR is resentful of CHARLIE's witness. CHARLIE anxious to offer reassurance. It is doomed to failure)

CHARLIE

Boss is always in the cafe at one o'clock.

ARTHUR	So bloody what. I don't care where he is. Boss knows how he's on wi' me. Not comin' round here checkin' every five minutes.
CHARLIE	Alright that way.
ARTHUR	Alright what way? What ye mean?
CHARLIE	Understands.
ARTHUR	Understands what?
CHARLIE	There'll be a bit o' waste.
ARTHUR	What ye talkin' about? Thirty five years I've worked here man! Wi should have an understandin'.
CHARLIE	Oh aye!
ARTHUR	Leaves it ti me.
CHARLIE	I wasn't meanin' nothin' like…
ARTHUR	Just gerron with your bait.
	(Pause. Reflectively munching. Drinking)
CHARLIE	Time's yor Gerald comin'?
ARTHUR	In his own time.
CHARLIE	Is 'e still on the same job?
ARTHUR	Not just on a job. He's a sales representative.
CHARLIE	Oh!
ARTHUR	Does business studies. Economics.
CHARLIE	Always been a big reader yor Gerald.
	(ARTHUR taps his brow)

ARTHUR   Got ti have it upstairs...

CHARLIE   Ye've always said, he was a big reader.

ARTHUR   Should never begrudge people that gets on in business.

CHARLIE   Oh! A don't begrudge them Arthur. No, A never do that... begrudge...

ARTHUR   I should think not. Not just work. It's economics.

CHARLIE   Like reckonin' up?

ARTHUR   More than that.

CHARLIE   A'm not bad at reckonin'...

ARTHUR   Not bad at pokin' yor fuckin' nose into what doesn't concern ye. I'll say that!

                (Pause)

                Anyhow, it's the words.

CHARLIE   What sort of words?

ARTHUR   Big words.

CHARLIE   Sort've big words?

ARTHUR   Aw man! You'd be none the wiser.

                (Pause)

                Capital Expenditure!

CHARLIE   Eh?

ARTHUR   Don't know what it means do ye?

CHARLIE   Not exactly.

ARTHUR   Well, there y' are then! Got ti know exactly.

CHARLIE	Oh!
ARTHUR	'Cos then ye can deal with things. When ye know exactly…
	(*Pause*)
CHARLIE	What's it mean then?
ARTHUR	Eh?
CHARLIE	Capital Expenditure!
ARTHUR	What's it mean? Well! It means, workin' out… findin' out, whatever it is ye want, then decidin' if it's worth havin', ye could buy it, if ye can afford it. Ye've got ti realise, there's different classes of money. There's big money, and little money. Capital expenditure is to do with big money…
CHARLIE	My reckonin' be no good then eh!
ARTHUR	Huh!
CHARLIE	A don't understand these things like you do Arthur.
ARTHUR	You look at that fish quay. You look what's happened down there. eh! Look at Northern Trawlers. Bankrupt! Eh! I mean who would've thought. Ye know what they've lost? Five million. Five bloody million!
CHARLIE	Shee! Ye bugga!
ARTHUR	How would ye like the worry o' that eh?
CHARLIE	Bloody awful!
ARTHUR	How would you feel, if ye'd lost five million.

CHARLIE   Bloody terrible.

ARTHUR   But somebody will have ti sort it out.

CHARLIE   How will the do that?

ARTHUR   Have to go through everythin'. Study how it got lost. It's all about economics. Wife's father once offered me two hundred pound ti set up on me own. A wouldn't touch it. Take on a debt like that. Never off yor back. Forms, documents. Man, there's people would get their eyes on that two hundred pound. Solicitors, estate agents, insurance men. Ye bugga, the' wouldn't sleep 'till they had it off ye… Then walk away, an' leave ye wi' the debt. Could've had me own business. Wife was keen. 'Sort yorsel' out', she said. *(ARTHUR throws away the dregs of his tea)* Ah! well, back ti the grind… *(He returns to skinning the last of the fillets)* You better get started sweepin' up.

                 (CHARLIE applies himself to the brush. With ARTHUR's back turned, CHARLIE works himself into a spot at the kiln door, where he can steal a couple of fish fillets. Popping them into a plastic bag, he sweeps over to his coat hanging on a nail, and transfers them into a pocket. Making sure ARTHUR is unaware. ARTHUR turns to just miss the action.

                 ARTHUR waves his knife despairingly indicating the ruin of the smokehouse)

ARTHUR   Look at it! It's obvious what they're doin'.

CHARLIE   What's that Arthur?

ARTHUR   Runnin' it down! That's what! Gettin' work done on the cheap. Clapped out machinery.

61

(Glaring at CHARLIE)

Unskilled labour...

(CHARLIE circles round behind ARTHUR. Finishing off the sweeping)

ARTHUR   When I started here, there was eighteen men, an' boys. Experienced curers, and filleters. The' got the work out of ye, but ye knew where ye stood. *(Lifting his head to observe CHARLIE)* Anybody didn't pull their weight... Out! Double quick! By God, were the' not! Straight out, bang! And I tell ye! By Christ! All that will have ti come back. Too much of it these days. People gettin' carried! Boss will have ti realise.

CHARLIE   Not a bad bloke really!

ARTHUR   *(Cynical)* Oh no! Meet 'm in the boozer. Stands ye a pint. Same bloke, give ye anythin' as long as it's not money.

(CHARLIE preparing to lay up his broom)

CHARLIE   About time for me off Arthur.

ARTHUR   But one day! Listen! You'll bloody see! He's gonna come round here, and ask me what's what. And I'll tell'm. You wait! You'll see. He's gonna say, "Arthur! What's needed round here?" "Some proper bloody help" I'll say! "For a start"... By God then there'll be a few changes. Will there not! Be round wi' the chopper then. Be a right sort out.

(The significance of the threat is not lost on CHARLIE)

CHARLIE   A've swept up!

ARTHUR   Have ye?

CHARLIE	Is there anythin' more A can do.
ARTHUR	Nowt as would be of use.
CHARLIE	Just get off then.
ARTHUR	Might as well.
	(CHARLIE goes to his coat, and slowly puts it on)
CHARLIE	What ye said Arthur! About me packin' in.
ARTHUR	Never said, 'pack in'.
CHARLIE	No! But ye asked us, if A wanted ti keep the job.
ARTHUR	Just a question.
CHARLIE	Well, A need ti keep it on.
ARTHUR	Up ti you.
CHARLIE	A couldn't get by. It's just part time. A'd do extra, but me back. Goes crack on us!
ARTHUR	Get on the sick.
CHARLIE	Oh! A'm not entitled ti sick. A've no cards. Like the boss says, if A earn more'n thirty quid, it just comes off me pension. So he just gives 's it in me hand. Saves the stamp!...
ARTHUR	Nowt ti do wi' me that.
CHARLIE	But ye'll be talkin' to him. Like when ye have ti tell him what's needed.
ARTHUR	It'll be up ti the boss.
CHARLIE	Aye! well! Just be off then... *(Begins to leave)* So long Arthur... *(Reaches the exit)*

ARTHUR	Charlie!
	(CHARLIE stops)
ARTHUR	Come here!
	(CHARLIE shuffles back. ARTHUR dips into his back pocket, brings out a couple of pounds. Gives it to CHARLIE)
ARTHUR	Here! Share of that cashers!
	(CHARLIE slow)
	Go on! Take it…
	(CHARLIE accepts)
CHARLIE	Eee! Thanks Arthur…Get mesel' a few tabs.
ARTHUR	That's what ye want ti pack in. The bloody smokin'…
CHARLIE	Right Arthur. Thanks!
	(CHARLIE shuffles again to the door)
CHARLIE	Tell ye what! A could come in sharp tomorrow. Give ye a hand wi' the packin'…
ARTHUR	Suit yorsel'…
	(The two FISHWIVES come out of their shed and resume their places at the bench)
CHARLIE	*(About to pass through the door)* Tirra then Arthur.
ARTHUR	Hey! A'll tell ye this. Ye come in the world wi' nowt an' that's what ye'll go out with… Just remember!
	(CHARLIE leaves)

Soft as shit! I dunno! I am! Soft as shit!

(*ARTHUR returns to his work*)

(*CHARLIE joins the two FISHWIVES. He tries to bum another cigarette from them*)

(*Offstage The imperative sound of a motor horn*)

(*ARTHUR stops his work, and closes to the pigeon basket. Lifting the lid, and fishing into it. GERALD approaches passing the FISHWIVES & CHARLIE*)

ARTHUR Come here! Come here ye twat!.

(*GERALD enters the smokehouse, and confronts his father at exactly the moment ARTHUR withdraws 'Stop Out Stanley' from the basket. ARTHUR confused. GERALD disapproving*)

ARTHUR A know! A know! A know what you're thinkin'. A'm stupid!

GERALD Aw man da!

ARTHUR Alright! Alright! But look, A'm not puttin' him in. A'm takin' him out.
O.K. you're right. He's a waste o' stake money.

GERALD Da! A wash me hands o' ye.

ARTHUR Aw! That's not nice. Don't say that son.

GERALD Don't be so bloody wet man. Just knock 'm...

ARTHUR You're right!

GERALD Knock 'm!

ARTHUR Has ti be done!

GERALD	Should've made yor mind ti that long ago.
	(GERALD reaches for the basket)
ARTHUR	Not easy!
GERALD	Don't be so daft. Simple as that.
	(GERALD demonstrates the pulling of a pigeon's neck. ARTHUR holds out the bird to him. GERALD responds by picking up the basket. Turns to leave)
GERALD	Yor bird da!
ARTHUR	Gerald!
GERALD	No time ti debate da. The bosses is waitin'...
	(He leaves. ARTHUR follows him to the door. Holding 'Stop Out Stanley'. Watching GERALD go)
ARTHUR	That's right son. Doesn't do ti keep the bosses waitin'...
	(ARTHUR holds the bird. GERALD exits past the two FISHWIVES & CHARLIE)
ARTHUR	*(Intimately to the pigeon)* Ye heard what the lad said. I mean, it's time an' money. Y' know! How it is! Not up ti me! Time an' money!...
	(Places his third, and fourth right hand finger round the pigeons throat, and prepares to pull its neck. The younger FISHWIFE averts her gaze. CHARLIE grins. The older FISHWIFE looks on impassively. Taking out her packet of cigarettes. Extracting one. ARTHUR becoming aware of their interest, puts his back between them and the action. Forces himself to the deed. He stops. Squints

at the bird. Lifting it nearer to his view).

ARTHUR   What's that? Eh? Ye got summick in yor eye? Let's have a look. *(Examining the bird. Rubbing his finger across its eyelid)* Aw! just a bit o' straw... There, it's out...

('Stop Out Stanley' seems to slip out of his hand. Soaring aloft.

Offstage. The creak of its wings. Its shadow traces over the ground and walls. The four heads of the spectators, lift and turn following the flight)

CHARLIE takes his chance to lift a cigarette out of the packet. The older FISHWIFE, raises a hand to clip his head. ARTHUR shrugs... everyone is smiling. Freeze)

FIN.

——— *The Long Line* ———

This play was first produced at Live Theatre Co, The Quayside, Newcastle in the summer of 1986.

Original Cast (Playing many roles)

Denise Bryson

Robson Green

Sammy Johnson

Val McLane

Annie Orwin

David Whitaker

Directed by Max Roberts

The photograph shows David Whitaker (left) and Robson Green singing a sea shanty.

PART ONE	'THE LOVE OF TWO BOYS'	1890
	George Pearson the First	
	Da Pearson	
	Ma Pearson	
	Cousin Molly	
	Preacher	

PART TWO	'THE SISTERS'	1930
	George Pearson the Second	
	Mr Purdy	
	Thompson	
	Sally	
	Elsie	
	Spanish Maria	
	1st Seaman	
	2nd Seaman	

PART THREE	'A BOY FROM SHIELDS'	1990
	George Pearson the Third (known as Digga)	
	Prison Officer	
	Betty	
	Andy	
	Linda	
	Kev (known as Grippa)	
	Natalie	
	Edna	
	Scampi Jack	
	Ray	

PART ONE

'The Love of Two Boys'

Cullercoats 1890

A.M. THE KITCHEN OF THE PEARSON COTTAGE.

	(MA PEARSON preparing a swill with baited hooks. A swill is a cane basket used to arrange the long line, and fish hooks. GEORGE enters. Collecting his jacket. Looking for his sea boots. His father calls to him)
DA *(O.S)*	Hey up lad! Let's be havin' ye. Be on here! Y'comin'?
	(GEORGE turns to his mother as if he would confide something)
MA	Go on wi' ye. Get ti yor da!
	(GEORGE carries on searching)
MA	S'marrer wi' ye? Ye hear him shoutin'. Get along!
GEORGE	Don't he ever think other people might know right from wrong?
MA	You tell 'm what's to yor mind then.
DA *(O.S)*	Come on son! Come on!
GEORGE	I try to tell 'm.
MA	Can be no secrets in this way George. You understand what I say?
GEORGE	Bein' pushed around!
MA	That's not true. Don' make that yor excuse. He don't do that. Whatever he says is done fatherly.
GEORGE	It's my life.

71

MA   Now you listen! You put this burden on me, and it's a burden I'll not have. I keep nowt from yor Da.

DA *(O.S)*   C'mon...! The tide's among the boats.

(GEORGE picks up his boots, and puts them under his arm. Collects a coil of rope. Puts it over his shoulder)

GEORGE   Feel like a dog.

MA   Talkin' nonsense. That's nonsense talk. You got a notion in yor head, then stand face ti yor da, an' have it out.

GEORGE   Only ti Shields Ma! Two mile down the road.

MA   It'd be like a dog ye'd go...

GEORGE   Ma!...

MA   A'm listenin' ti no more...

GEORGE   Just sayin'...

MA   Wisht!

(Enter DA)

DA   C'mon then! What's the hold up?

GEORGE   Findin' me boots...

DA   An' A've put the sea anchor aboard, the dan, the bobbins, an' reels, an' were ye leavin' it ti yor owld da ti push her off the beach, while ye were lookin' for your boots?

GEORGE   Couldn't find 'm.

DA   But you've gottem under yor arm, an' look you've got the toes pointin' up again.

GEORGE   Aw man da!

72

DA	*(To MA)* Am I tellin' him? How many times eh? *(To GEORGE)* Ye carry your sea boots under yor arm, allus make sure the toes is pointin' down.
GEORGE	For why?
DA	For why? A tell ye for why. Think of a drowned man bein' carried ashore, an' which whay would his toes be pointin'?
	(GEORGE thinks about it. Then twists the toes of his boots to point down)
DA	Y'see! Always go out the way ye mean to come back son. Now c'mon!
	(GEORGE hesitant. Looks to his MA)
DA	An' ye got all yor gear? 'Cos there's no comin' back for what ye forget. That's another thing son. It'd be a sign from heaven ye were never meant ti sail.
	(DA leaves. Taking the swill of hooks. A last glance to MA, and GEORGE follows)
MA	*(To herself)* An' it's all the years on an open deck for the wind ti scatter thor brains.

• • • •

BEFORE THE ENTRANCE TO MOLLY's COTTAGE.

(MOLLY is baiting hooks. She sings while she works)

MOLLY	'Blow the Wind Southerly' etc.
	(Enter MA PEARSON, like the arrival of winter. The song dies)
MOLLY	Oh hello Aunty Pearson.
MA	Mornin' ti ye.

73

MOLLY	What a nice surprise. How are ye?
MA	Keep ti yor work lassie!
MOLLY	An' how's me Uncle Pearson?
MA	Managin'.
MOLLY	That's nice. A'm glad ti hear that.
	(MA circles MOLLY studying her)
MOLLY	Well A've no present troubles mesel'. Not ti speak of. In fact A'm very well... Thank ye. Plenty ti keep us busy...
	(MA suddenly thrusts a present into MOLLY's hands)
MA	Here A've brought ye this.
MOLLY	Eee. Well! Whatever?
MA	It's a present.
MOLLY	For me? *(Fumbles the wrapping)*
MA	Don't bother openin' it. A can tell ye what it is without ye openin' it.
	(MOLLY puts down the parcel. Carries on working)
MA	It was one o' me mother's best plates.
MOLLY	Eee. But Aunty Pearson.
MA	Ye once took a fancy to it.
MOLLY	The one wi' the roses...
MA	Not summick I'd lightly part wi'.
MOLLY	The green leaves round the edge.
MA	What's family is not easy given up.

MOLLY	Oh! But thank ye kindly Aunty Pearson.
	(Pause)
MA	The crack! Is only very slight.
MOLLY	Oh great care I'd take of it. Thank you Aunty Pearson, it's a lovely surprise. Yes! Er… George, and Uncle Pearson will be off are the'?
MA	By the fore tide.
MOLLY	Still ti the long line?
MA	Aye! The long line.
MOLLY	Not changin' over ti the drift (net).
MA	Ye know how it is wi' the sea, an' the moods o' men, they'll be feelin' each other out.
MOLLY	That's true.
MA	But if it was me, A never waste time. Not when me mind is set to a purpose.
MOLLY	No!
MA	Molly!
MOLLY	Aunty Pearson?
MA	Tell me lassie. Are ye courtin'?
MOLLY	Courtin' Aunty Pearson?
MA	Isn't that what A said?
MOLLY	Yes… but…
MA	Can ye not answer the question?
MOLLY	A don't know what ye mean Aunty Pearson.

MA   A mean nowt would surprise me about the devious nature of men... or wimmen!

MOLLY   A'm took up wi' no man Aunty Pearson.

MA   But wasn't yor Cousin Annie took up wirra pitman, and nobody knowin'!
          'Til the nights drew out, an' the' tossed him ower a cliff.
          Ye can live one end of a street, an' not know what's goin' on at the other.

MOLLY   A've never been courted Aunty Pearson.

MA   No! I'm surprised. To have reached yor age! An wi' such obvious qualities.

MOLLY   Thank ye Aunty Pearson.

MA   Ye have a good name lassie. Ti be baitin' a thousand hooks between tides.
          Good legs, an' good shoulders!
          Aye! Yor Aunty Lisle said ye could carry a creel as would cripple a donkey.
          Ye wonder what men want!

· · · ·

THE COBLE AT SEA.

(GEORGE is aft at the tiller. Controlling the Jib. DA is forward paying out the line)

DA   Keep her round! Keep her round! That's it. Steady! Tighten the jib.
          Steady!
          Aye. Ye were sayin'...

GEORGE   It's an invention Da.

DA   Invention?

GEORGE   The beam trawl.

DA   Oh!

GEORGE	Mr Purdy in Shields has invented it.
DA	Shields eh! Keep her round!
GEORGE	Idea is to draw this bag along the sea bed.
DA	Watch yor mark son, watch it. Take it from the headland, an' keep her round.
GEORGE	The mouth is kept open wi' the beam.
DA	Steady now! Steady on the line!
GEORGE	An' it scrapes up all the bottom livin' fish.
DA	Hard over. Harder! Bring her away.
GEORGE	Y'see Da…
DA	Fish son, is like people. The' live in toons, and villages. Ye should try an' understand that.
GEORGE	How the' intend ti pull it is with a paddle steamer.
DA	Jus' like folks ashore! A'm tellin' ye. Fish come tigether in places where the' prosper.
GEORGE	Lot o' power in them paddles Da. Reckon a single drag would haul in two ton.
DA	An' just like people, what fish can't abide is great, and sudden distrubance. Are ye watchin' yor mark?
GEORGE	Aye Da!
DA	Keep her round. Keep her round. I think we might've took a fastener!
	(Pulls hard on the line)
DA	Come away there. Come away. Keep her head round. That's it. She's away. That's it.

(The line is freed)

DA   Aye! A beam trawl eh!

GEORGE   Aye Da!

DA   Scrapin' the sea bed?

GEORGE   Aye Da.

DA   That'd be a mucky business. Take her ahead!

GEORGE   Aye Da!

DA   No son! The long line! That's the tried and trusty way. Just yor little hook, a birra bait, an' easy the' come.

• • • •

MA PEARSON & MOLLY AS BEFORE

MA   A've said to him, "George son, ye'll not always have yor Ma."

MOLLY   Right!

MA   "Ye should be lookin' around."

MOLLY   He's a fine lad Aunty Pearson.

MA   But he says, "Ma!" "Ma!" he says. "Where would I ever find the equal ti yoursel'?"

MOLLY   Eee! That's nice.

MA   "Yes," I said, "That's true son, for as God's me judge, ye have ti be careful".

MOLLY   Oh! True!

MA   He suffers you see...
            From a terrible natural shyness.

MOLLY   Does 'e?

MA   There's an impediment that puts some men ti untold sufferin'.

MOLLY   I mind poor Herbie Lisle.

MA   What about Herbie Lisle?

MOLLY   Suffered for a week.

MA   What was that?

MOLLY   Not wantin' ti ask for help.

MA   Herbie Lisle?

MOLLY   Terrible inflammation.

MA   From what?

MOLLY   This spelk in his backside.

MA   There now.

MOLLY   A understand what ye mean Aunty Pearson.

MA   A wonder. Anyhow, some men is marked out.

MOLLY   Aye.

MA   Aye, an' there's been this damned invention.

MOLLY   Invention?

MA   Some man in Shields has invented a contraption, an' isn't George of the mind ti seek employment with 'm.

MOLLY   To leave his Da?

MA   Aye!

MOLLY   Not ti leave his Da!

MA   Aye ti leave his Da, an' me.

MOLLY   Would ye believe it.

MA   A'd not have believed it.

MOLLY   Oh Aunty Pearson.

MA   An' for what? Ti live in dirty lodgins.

MOLLY   Oh no!

MA   In the Dockwray Square of Shields...

MOLLY   Dear me!

MA   Wi' all them feckless people.

MOLLY   What he might fall into.

MA   Some nasty, dye haired, red moothed, ha'penny fanny, that couldn't gut a fish.

MOLLY   That'd be wicked.

MA   Of course it'd be wicked.

MOLLY   I'm sorry ti hear it.

MA   Aye!

MOLLY   Eee! Aunty Pearson, if there's anythin' A can do.

MA   Well y' know as well as me lassie.
Fisherlad must marry fisherlass, or he might as well cut off his right arm.

MOLLY   Such a waste.

MA   Just for bein' backward in comin' forward.

MOLLY   Mevves his Da will talk him out of it.

MA   Cannit rely on seamen when they're ashore.
It's summick ti do wi' balance.
No lassie! Here's a matter us wimmin has ti take into our own hands.

MOLLY	How di ye mean Aunty Pearson?
MA	Molly Pearson! Our George needs a wife.
	(Pause. The significance dawns on MOLLY)
MOLLY	But Aunty Pearson, what ye sayin'?
MA	It's clear enough what A'm sayin'.
MOLLY	A'm his full cousin! A have the same name.
MA	This place is swarmin' wi' Pearsons. Thor's not a half a dozen surnames in this village. Aren't wi all mixed up.
MOLLY	Aunty Pearson!
MA	A would've thought the propostition would've been of interest.
MOLLY	A don't know what ti say. A really don't.
MA	Are ye tellin' us, it doesn't meet wi' yor favour?
MOLLY	A didn't say that. Did A? A don't know. A'm just taken aback.
MA	Well say summick.
MOLLY	A wouldn't know what to say. A mean what would George say?
MA	He'd be... encouraged.
MOLLY	But A mean, he's just twenty year old, an' well... A'm thirty...
MA	Two!
MOLLY	Yes! Well!
MA	Might make for two of us feelin' a bit desperate.

MOLLY	Aunty Pearson, it's a strange thing yor suggestin'.
MA	It's a fair propostition.
MOLLY	All the same, A need time ti think. A mean, what if George... Y' know! A mean, don't ye think we should wait a while, an' see what happens?
MA	Don't ye think ye've waited long enough?

• • • •

THE COBLE

(GEORGE and DA are rowing for home)

DA	*(In rythm with the stroke)* Aye tigether! Aye tigether! No son, the sea bed, it's like a garden. Tigether! An' this beam trawl, draggin' itsel' over the ground that feeds the fish. Tigether! Breakin' it up. Crushin' the shells. Uprootin' the plants. What'd be the outcome?
GEORGE	Y' see Da.
DA	Tigether! Pull away! Haul away! No Son, the long line keeps a balance. Takin' only what ye need. Leavin' the young ti grow.
GEORGE	But Da!
DA	Gill net, for by the herrin' come, but...
GEORGE	Mr Purdy...
DA	Now listen Son! There's eighty cobles workin' outa this harbour. Has been for more years than anybody can remember. An every season known, an kept.

Cod, haddock or sprat. That's eighty families, fathers, sons, mothers, dowters, all wi' gud employment.

GEORGE   But A'm sayin' Mr Purdy.

DA   Mr Purdy!... Here ship oars.
One... two... inboard!

(They relax from the rowing)

DA   Mr Purdy! Has he worked out what he's gonna do wi' two ton o' haddocks?

GEORGE   Likely as sell them.

DA   Then another drag, another two ton.

GEORGE   Like as not.

DA   Then another paddle steamer?

GEORGE   Powerful boats Da!

DA   Burnin' all that coal.

GEORGE   Aye Da.

DA   Outa Shields?

GEORGE   For the deeper anchorage.

DA   Workcd it all out have the'?

GEORGE   Was in the Shield's 'Gazette'.

DA   Ideas always look good on paper son, but show me the book, that tells ye how ti skin a skate.

GEORGE   Could be the comin' thing Da.

DA   Tell ye this for nowt son. Yor Mr Purdy will fill his docks wi' fish that nobody wants, an' nobody can afford.

GEORGE	It'd be openin' up the sea Da!
DA	More likely turn it into a desert. Sort've invention would that be? Here!

(He hands GEORGE his brass telescope)

DA	There's yor granda's glass. A fine instrument. Ground, and founded in brass by a craftsman. 'George Pearson 1852'. Take a look thro' it. Go on, search out the horizon.

(Does as he is instructed)

DA	How does it do?
GEORGE	Fine Da.
DA	Pulls it near?
GEORGE	Very near Da!
DA	But not beyond!
GEORGE	Course not!
DA	Takes ye ti the horizon, an' no further. That's all ye want from an invention.

(GEORGE closes down the telescope, hands it back to his DA)

DA	No, you keep it. It's yor's now. A give it ti ye.
GEORGE	Thanks Da!
DA	Yes! Take care of it. Let it remind ye of... limitations! C'mon... dip oars! *(They resume the rowing)*

Tigether!	Pull!	
	Tigether!	Haul away!
	Tigether!	Pull. Tigether.

• • • •

THE SHORE. EVENING. DARKENING DOWN.

(*MA PEARSON comes forward with a lantern.
Puts it down, and faces the sea. Folding her arms.
Drawing her shawl tight around her. MOLLY
appears above, and behind. She is on higher ground,
and holds her lantern on a pole*)

(*MOLLY sings*)

MOLLY   None but us ti rue their loss,
If they should not come yem,
Those warm abed
They divven fuss,
'Tis aal the same ti them.

So hold yor lantern high lad,
Hold yor lantern high,
Ti catch yor daddie's eye lad,
Ti catch yor daddie's eye.

Any sign Aunty Pearson?

MA   Nowt but the black water.

MOLLY   Must be nigh on.

MA   Are ye in line wi' the point?

MOLLY   I am.

MA   An' yor lantern high?

MOLLY   It is…

(*MOLLY sets the pole and lantern into the ground.
Comes forward to a position closer to MA. Both
women strain to see across the harbour entrance*)

MA   Two sons A had, but one the sea took!
Ti put its dark blanket about his head.
Mornin' an' night A walked this shore.
Mornin' an' night, for the turnin' of both tides.
Hopin' it would tire of his keepin'.
An' brush, an' a comb a brought ti tidy the sand

from his hair.
But it was denied me lassie.
That little mercy was denied me.
My God!
Because we call it home.
What comfortless places wi cling to.
Is the light safe?

MOLLY   *(Glancing back)* Aye! It's well stood.

MA   Then A think... maybe one day!
Some child at play, pilin' sand, will maybes get a little joy ti decorate its top wi' some small piece of whitened bone.
D'ye think that Molly?
Then maybe in that knowin' way of children, will take it home for treasure.
Some little fragment come back to cheer us out of that cold nature.

MOLLY   Look! Ahead! Ahead there! Beyond the channel! There's white water breakin'.

MA   Di ye see that?

MOLLY   A think A see that.

MA   Come on then! Come to us bonny lads.

MOLLY   Now I see them. I see them.

MA   An' is it steep? Be the entrance, is the water pilin' up?

MOLLY   Comin' thro'. Thor comin' thro'.

MA   C'mon me hinnies!

MOLLY   It's them. They're clearin' the scarp.

MA   Pull ti wi! Pull ti wi!

MOLLY   *(Picking up the lantern and swinging it)* Ahoy!

MA	Aye ye dark grumblin' beast, give us wor men... Ye've met yor match. My name is Mother!
MOLLY	Thro' ti the channel. They're thro'!
MA	Ye wonder eh! How wimmin live in this uncertainty.
MOLLY	Thro' ti the flat water now! Thro' ti the flat water Aunty Pearson.
MA	Aye luv! A see them! A see them!

(Begins to move to the water's edge)

MOLLY	Aunty Pearson!

(MA stops)

MA	What is it lassie?
MOLLY	A'm agreeable! If it's still yor wish for George an' me. A'm agreeable.
MA	Are ye! Well take my place. Go on down an' lend yorsel' ti haul them ashore.
MOLLY	But George, an' me, how is it to be done?
MA	Make yorsel' available.
MOLLY	But how will he study me intention?
MA	Wade in up ti yor neck!

(MOLLY flies off like caution to the wind. MA pickes up the lantern, waits)

MA	An' timorrow, I'll keep ye a place i' the Chapel.

• • • •

THE CHAPEL. INT. A.M.

(Hymn... 'For Those In Peril On The Sea' GEORGE and MOLLY sit uncomfortably between MA and DA Pearson. The Preacher in plain fisherman's gansey, holds his bible in one hand, offering the benediction. The hymn ends. They sit)

PREACHER   Brethren! No man having drunk old wine desireth the new. For straightaway he sayeth, 'Verily the old is the best'.
Luke, Chapter five, verse thirty nine.

(MA nods in agreement. Glances knowingly to MOLLY)

PREACHER   Lord! Help us ti understand thy words, that we may keep to a true course.
Brethren! We are but a simple folk. Huddled tigether at this raw edge of land, and sea.

(MA nudges MOLLY closer to GEORGE)

PREACHER   Yet our dwellings are strong, and built upon His Rock, and will endure the ragin' storm.
Then leave not yor father's house!

(Pausing to allow the significance to sink into GEORGE)

PREACHER   Verily I say unto you, 'The old is the best'.
But Brethren, it is not just of wine! It is not just of the Tempest, and the storm. Remember also the Temptation!
For those who are young are beset!
Their voyage is but at a beginning, and the Temptation is uncharted.
Brethren! Not far from our door is the town built above the Black Middens.
There are the shiftless people, havin' no settled condition to their lives.
In that place are the strange practices of men, brought from the lands of heat, and desolation.
And the sickness for which there is no cure... besets them.

Yet Brethren, they are full of *inventions*, and distractions, to tempt the unwary.
Oh! Lord, let not our young men be caught up.
Let not the coloured lights, an' musical discords bemuse the eyes, an' ears of our children.
For in that place is no shelter from the Storm.
For is not a Shiel, but a crude making of sticks, and mud.
And the North, and the South Shiel's will not prevail, nor stand before the wind, and rain.
Lord! Their dwellings tumble about them, and have no permanence.
Let then our young men keep their present hearth, and company. Remembering the family is the anchor of their lives.
For here is our security, and salvation.
Brethren! Comfort each other with yor hearts, and warm each other wi' yor bodies.
So will the Lord be with you always.
Amen!

TOGETHER	Amen!

(A meditative prayer. The service is over)

PREACHER	Well George, ye took five baskets yesterday.
DA	Mostly codlin'...

(MA is having a quiet word with MOLLY and GEORGE, who leave the Chapel together)

PREACHER	No flatties?
DA	Not a sign o' flatties.
PREACHER	Our lass was sayin'. Being pestered for lemon soles.
DA	She will be... Yes. She will be! Where's yor lass carryin'?
PREACHER	Whitley!
DA	Ah! Big properties up there.

(Rejoined by MA)

MA	Lovely words Minister. Lovely words.
PREACHER	Thank ye.
MA	Ye get right inside. Ye do! Right inside.
PREACHER	Thank ye Mother Pearson.
MA	Yor doin' the Lord's work.
DA	It'll be a good class o' trade Whitley! eh?
PREACHER	O aye! Very good class.
MA	That's nice.
DA	Birra debt though is there?
PREACHER	Well! Aye, there is a birra debt.
DA	A thought there'd be a birra debt.
PREACIIER	Payin' monthly.
DA	But the money's there?
PREACHER	O aye! The money's there. The' just don't like er...
DA	Partin'...
PREACHER	Handlin' it...!
MA	Aye!
DA	Minister says they're cryin' out for lemon soles in Whitley.
MA	I stick ti Percy Main y'know!
DA	Pit folk!
MA	Haddocks, an' dabs!

DA   Wimmin wi' shawls around thor heads, the money's on the dot.

MA   An' when the' spend, thor bellies comes first.

DA   Love thor crabs! Bigger the better!

MA   Clean 'm thorsel's. No bother…

PREACHER   Oh' Whitley Bay! Little crabs…

MA   So A've heard…

PREACHER   Want them dressed.

DA   Them big hooses. Y'know what the' say. 'Bigger the hoose…'

PREACHER   'Smaller the pantry'. Yes, food for thought George! A'll hev a word wi' the missus.

             (They walk off)

· · · ·

GEORGE AND MOLLY REPAIR A LONG LINE AT THE FORESHORE.

(Replacing the snoods, and hooks. Snood is the lateral branch that carries the hook away from the main line)

GEORGE   No need y'know. A can manage.

MOLLY   Don't mind George!

GEORGE   Just 'cos she's talked you into it.

MOLLY   She's not talked me into it. A like helpin' ye.
             Woulda helped ye anyways.
             Pass that cordin'…
             How would ye have got it all done anyhow?
             The long line! The tangle of it!
             Gets langer, an' langer!
             Anyhow A'd be doin' nowt else.

(Pause)

GEORGE	A'm not daft y'know!
MOLLY	Course yor not.
GEORGE	They mus' think A'm daft. Do you think A'm daft?
MOLLY	A don't think yor daft George.
GEORGE	A know what yor up to. C'mon! A'm not deaf, an' blind!
MOLLY	What ye sayin'?
GEORGE	A'm not stupid. A know what yor after.
MOLLY	George...
GEORGE	An' that Holy Willie, wi' his bible blather. A know what she's up to. A know what she's tryin' ti get ye to do.
MOLLY	Di ye?
GEORGE	Makin' it so obvious! She wants ye ti talk me outa goin' to Shields don' she?
MOLLY	Ye should think about things.
GEORGE	Well, A'm tellin' ye now. A'll not be stopped. Ye might as well know that.
MOLLY	Shoulda greased this cord. It's far too brittle.

(Pause)

GEORGE	Gonna tell ye summick Molly! Summick A've wanted ti tell ye for a long time. When me brother was drowned... A knew...! A knew about... you an' him.

(MOLLY stops working)

GEORGE

It's alright! A never telled anyone.
A mean A was just a kid.
A seen ye's kissin'! A couldn't help it!
A wasn't spyin'. Then afterwards. Wi' him an'
me sleepin' in the same bed.
A think he wanted ti talk about it.
Like needed ti tell somebody. Like he was happy!
A thought it was great, me big brother lettin' us
on a secret. He said A hadn't got ti tell nobody...
about you an' him...
An' well! A never did.
But ye loved him didn't ye? Our Danny!
Is that why ye've never courted since?
A loved him as well y'see. But A can understand
how ye felt.
Ye'll think this is daft, but A'll tell ye...
The night he was drowned. A wanted ti come ti
ye.
A wanted ti come, and give ye a cuddle.
Well, A knew how upset ye'd be. A wanted ti
tell ye A knew.

(He pauses... They embrace... MOLLY distressed...)

GEORGE

A wanted ti put me arms around ye Molly. For
a bit o' comfort...
Then A was growin' up...
Well A wanted ti grow up, an' take his place wi'
ye...
Isn't it stupid what goes on in a kid's head.
"When A grow up Ma. A'm gonna marry Molly
Pearson"...
A think A must've put the idea in her head that
I was in love wi' ye.
Did she ever tell ye?
Y'know sometimes A get the idea she's tryin' ti
push us two tigether.
A mean, di ye get that impression?
As if ye'd ever fancy a kid like me.

(They kiss quite passionately. Part)

MOLLY

George! You've never had sisters! An' ye've
never seen a girl's body have ye?

93

GEORGE   No!

MOLLY   A've brothers! A'm used ti brothers. A know
                how the' think about girls.
                A'd not talk you out of yor purpose George!
                Not for yor Ma, or for me. You go to Shields wi'
                my blessin'…
                But by the North Cliff, the grass is long, an' fine
                for tumblin' into.
                An' fine comfort there'd be, in just lyin' there,
                like in a nest, wi' only the clouds for witness.
                An' finer comfort still d'ye not think… in that
                cuddle that's been saved up thro' all those
                months, an' years…

                (They leave… locked together…)

                • • • •

                THE LIVING ROOM OF THE COTTAGE.

                *(Eight weeks later. MA sits reading her bible. DA
                dressed for outdoors, looks out the window)*

MA   "Put not new wine into old bottles, or the bottle
                will burst.'
                Ahh!
                Ye can find anythin' in these black covers.

DA   The wind is freshenin' from the Sou' East.

MA   A door ye can keep open. Nothin' more than that.

DA   Be night it'll tug every loose end.

                (MA closes her bible)

MA   It's not the law ye should love ye children.
                There's no written law ti that.
                The love the' deserve is the only love ye should
                give. That's how I see it.

DA   Notice the Redshank, an' Dunlin comin' above
                the tide…

MA	All that was natural was given him. Everythin'. Well, he's said 'goodbye' to his luck now…
DA	Somethin' in that sky disturbs them.

(MA crosses over to him, and helps button his jacket)

MA	An' forbearin' ti smack his backside has been as much ti bother. That's my view.
DA	A pegged the boat ti the high mark. Maybe tigether we can pull it clear. It'll need ti be done!

(He turns to leave. Enter MOLLY)

MA	You take care now. D'ye hear me George Pearson, you take care…

(DA pauses…)

DA	It's true isn't it! The son who is lost gives less pain, than the one who leaves ye…

(He leaves with a slight acknowledging of MOLLY)

MA	*(Calling after him)* I'll be along. I'll be following. Just take care!
MOLLY	No word then?
MA	Eight weeks now. I think we can take it as meanin' he has put himself out of reach.
MOLLY	I'm sorry Aunty Pearson.
MA	Thee've nowt ti sorry for! What thee've never had, thee never miss.
MOLLY	Would ye like the fire backed? I can fetch some wood…
MA	The' were good boys. Both my sons. Warm, lovin' boys.

I can thank God I had the best o' them.
Comfortin' an' carin'…
Tears, an' smiles…
That's the joy of it. To be the one the' come runnin' to.
Clutchin' yor apron for refuge.

MOLLY   I'll take the basket down for wood, an' give
Uncle Pearson a hand to beachin' the coble.

MA   Beautiful they were. In their growin' days.
Beautiful in their limbs, an' hair an' breath.

MOLLY   Bide the fire now, an' leave it to me to help him…

MA   In all their huggin' an' nursin', there was such a
heat!

(MOLLY moves to leave. Pausing. Turns…)

MOLLY   A know how ye feel Aunty Pearson!

MA   How can ye?
How can ye know?
Not havin' had the love of two such boys!

End of Part One

PART TWO
'The Sisters'

1930

THE INNER OFFICE OF G. PURDY TRAWLERS LTD.

(The Managing Director, GEORGE PURDY, arranges himself behind his desk. His Chief Clerk, THOMPSON, stands in attendance. They both put on their bowler hats. It is like a court martial)

PURDY   You ready Thompson? Got the envelope? Right! Let him in, then stand to where you are.

THOMPSON   Sir!

PURDY   Just a minute! The drink? Is he with the drink?

THOMPSON   He's upright Mr Purdy, sir!

PURDY   Is he! Oh! Right then...
Well, get on with it.

(Clerk goes to the door, admits GEORGE)

THOMPSON   This way.

(GEORGE enters. Taking up a slightly swaying position in front of the desk. The clerk standing to oneside. PURDY reads a document as though in studied indifference, then finally looks up)

PURDY   Pearson!

GEORGE   Mr Purdy!

PURDY   This is not a pleasant duty.

GEORGE   All I've got to say is...

PURDY   Now hold on! Hold on! You are in my office, and when you are in my office, you first of all listen to me...

GEORGE	Eh?
PURDY	It is brought to my notice, by my officer, that you defy a clear…
GEORGE	Defy?
PURDY	I am saying, defy a clear command to put yourself aboard.
GEORGE	Mr Purdy…!
PURDY	A clear command to put yourself aboard…
GEORGE	The bilges was disgustin'…
PURDY	My vessels, George Pearson, are sea worthy vessels.
GEORGE	Hold on!
PURDY	And any suggestion from you to the contrary, and I will bring an action that will take from you every penny you posses.
GEORGE	A possess three, an' sixpence between me, an' the next settlin'! Mr Purdy.
PURDY	Don't compound your behaviour with insolence Pearson.
GEORGE	A'm compounded wi' debt Mr Purdy. Now is it my turn ti speak?
PURDY	You signed the log…
GEORGE	Not arguin' about signin' the log.
PURDY	And therefore signatory to the Articles of the Merchant Navy Shipping Act.
	(THOMPSON nods vigorously in agreement. Which distracts GEORGE)

GEORGE	Hey Noddy! *(Mimics the nod)* Ye wanna keep off the strong ale.
PURDY	Merchant Navy Shipping Act...
GEORGE	Mister Purdy...!
PURDY	Upon which your failure to put yourself aboard...
GEORGE	*(To THOMPSON)* Wearin' a dut doesn't make ye Stanley Baldwin...
PURDY	Put yourself aboard at the lawful command of the ship's husband, captain or owner...
GEORGE	Look Mr Purdy, A'm in drink.
PURDY	Carries not only the penalty of fine, but of imprisonment. Furthermore.
GEORGE	It's a different argument when yor in drink...
PURDY	Furthermore...
GEORGE	The bilges was sluicin' watta...
PURDY	What did you say to the ship's husband?
GEORGE	Red lead, an' rust between us an' eternity Mr Purdy...
PURDY	What did you say... ?
GEORGE	Even the rats is shippin' out...
PURDY	What did you say to the ship's husband?
GEORGE	I told him to hadaway an' shite!
PURDY	The envelope! Give 'm the envelope!
	(THOMPSON thrusts the envelope into GEORGE's hand)

GEORGE   What's this like?

PURDY   It's your settling Pearson!

GEORGE   Settling?

PURDY   Four pounds, three shillings, and ninepence.

THOMPSON   Including liver, and roe monies!

GEORGE   Watta comin' thro' the for'd bulkhead, A was
                only pointin' out...

PURDY   Now get out!

GEORGE   Eh!

PURDY   You've got your settling...

GEORGE   What y'mean settlin'? Four pun', three an' nine-
                pence? For nineteen days, fishin' Faroe, an'
                Shetland!

THOMPSON   Less the subs! Less the subs!

GEORGE   What y'ron about? Subs!

PURDY   Your are not getting the drift Pearson. That is a
                final settlement.

GEORGE   Y'what?

PURDY   In fact I've been generous. I've added a pound.
                To get yourself a good pair of boots. A good pair
                of boots man, because when you leave here, you
                are going to do a lot of walking.

GEORGE   Ye givin' us the chop? Is that what you're doin'?

PURDY   You are casual labour Pearson.

GEORGE   I'm what?

PURDY   We are simply not re-engaging you.

GEORGE   Casual labour? I've sailed the Agnes Purdy
                nigh of six year. Casual labour?
                An' was me Da casual labour? Twenty five year
                wi' this company. An' me Granda...

PURDY   Take your settling Pearson...

GEORGE   My Grandfather was in the first crew of the first
                paddle steamer your Father....

THOMPSON   Come along Pearson...

GEORGE   You show 'm. Fifty year! Ye'll have records...

PURDY   Incitement! That's what you were at, incitement!

GEORGE   Casual labour?

PURDY   If you approach crewmen with the intention of
                causing discontent...

GEORGE   Oh! that's it is it? Not allowed ti complain are
                we?

THOMPSON   You have your settling. Mr Purdy is...

GEORGE   Aw! Shut your hole! Listen, yous don' bother
                me. Yor not the only trawler owners in Shields.

PURDY   Every owner in this port, for your information
                Pearson...

GEORGE   Who di ye think y'are, fuckin' Mussolini?

THOMPSON   That's enough!

PURDY   For your information! Is in the North East Coast
                Fishing Vessel Owners Association...

GEORGE   This is still a free country...

PURDY   With which organisation your name is now
                blackened...

GEORGE   Y'what?

PURDY	You will never work in Shields again... Now get out!
	(GEORGE moves to the door)
GEORGE	Ye've not heard the last of George Pearson...
	(Leaves. THOMPSON follows... Closing the door. Purdy sighs with relief)
(O.S)	*(The sound of a scuffle... Purdy listens at the door:)*
(O.S)	*(The sound of a thump...)*
PURDY	*(Cautiously at the door)* Thompson!

• • • •

THE HARBOUR VIEW.

(At separate stations three young women publicly proclaim their position)

ELSIE	*(Secretary of the National Unemployed Workers Movement. Her banner reads: "Down with the means test" NUWM)*
SALLY	*(Evangelist. Her placard reads: 'The Gospel Preached in the Free Gardiners Hall' No Collection)*
SPANISH MARIA	*(Prostitute, Walks the Street)*
	(A few unemployed loungers hang around)
SALLY	You might as well start Elsie.
ELSIE	Might as well! Comrades, friends... Until such time as the means of production shall be in the hands of the labouring classes...
	(GEORGE wanders into view. He carries his small kit bag. Disconsolate he stops to listen)

ELSIE   There will be no end to this misery.
               Eleven years ago. Lloyd George promised you a
               land fit for heroes.
               Look at it...
               Walk along Saville Street, what do you see?
               The debris of the Somme, limbless & blind, beg-
               ging for pennies.

SALLY   What about the slums?

ELSIE   Slums! In this town, four out of ten families live
               in two rooms or less...
               They live with middens, and standpipes, one tap
               between twenty families.

SALLY   Rats and rotten floorboards!

ELSIE   Absolutely right sister! While your Liberal coun-
               cillors hum and haw about the cost of Municipal
               housing, and their smug friends fill the columns
               of the Shields Daily News with letters.
               "Oh a family can live well enough on fifteen shil-
               lings a week".

SALLY   What about the unemployed?

ELSIE   Hmmmm! (*Clears her throat*) The unem... (*Gags*)
               Have you got them pastilles Sally?

SALLY   In your bag Elsie!

ELSIE   Not be a minute... (*Rummages her bag*)

               (*SALLY approaches GEORGE. Offering a tract*)

SALLY   Excuse me! Would you like to hear the word of
               Jesus?

GEORGE   Y'what?

SALLY   Our loving Saviour! Would you like to hear?

GEORGE   Not right now. Not the way I'm fixed. Don't
               think Jesus could help.

SALLY   Oh but he can. Ye've had some trouble haven't
                 ye? When I saw yor face I thought, that poor
                 man, he's troubled.

GEORGE   Well, I've jus' been kicked outa me job!

SALLY   Ah!

GEORGE   Kicked outa me lodgin's!

SALLY   Ah!

GEORGE   Kicked outa the Low Lights Tavern!

SALLY   Oh!

GEORGE   Could say I'm troubled.

SALLY   Come ye who are heavy laden...

GEORGE   I'm sure ye mean well pet, but you're talkin' to
                 a lost soul...

SALLY   "He who is lost is found again", Luke chapter
                 fifteen...

                 (Spanish MARIA suanters up)

MARIA   Hello George! Fancy a jam sandwich?

                 *(Saunters on, but stops to archly regard him over
                 her shoulder...)*

ELSIE   *(Coughs)* Hu'u'um! Where was I?

SALLY   The unemployed!

ELSIE   They give you a figure of one and three quarter
                 million. What they don't count, if you are taken
                 off the dole. Oh this is a reduction in labour. But
                 the Means Test takes you off the dole in six
                 months. Comrades, the real figure of unem-
                 ployment is nearer four million. They hide that
                 from you...

GEORGE	She's right!
SALLY	There is a Divine purpose George. That is your name? *(To ELSIE)* What about the Means Test?
ELSIE	Exactly! Whose idea was that?
LOUNGER	Bloody Labour!
ELSIE	Yes my friend! Those who have betrayed their class have found a place in this infamous National Government... But first the struggle is for bread...
GEORGE	Hear hear!
ELSIE	And justice!
GEORGE	Hear hear!
SALLY	I see the hand of God in everything...
MARIA	Hey George! You comin'...?
ELSIE	Comrades in this town, your children go hungry, and half a mile down this road they are dumping fish...
GEORGE	That's right! I've seen that...
LOUNGER	We've got to tighten our belts...
ELSIE	Like the Duke of Northumberland I suppose. Who says he finds five cars too many, so he's going to make do with four...
GEORGE	That's a good 'n...
ELSIE	But the Percys dine in satin dresses, and spend as much on a single meal as could keep a working man, and his family for a month... That is the nature of capitalism.

(But the loungers are drifting away)

MARIA	Hey George! What you doin'?
ELSIE	The Worker! Read the Daily Worker! Here! *(She begins to distribute the 'Worker'. Chasing after a departing lounger...)*
ELSIE	Read the Worker!
SALLY	If you've no lodging...
GEORGE	I think me friend's waiting miss!
SALLY	The Seamans Hostel, 52 Duke Street...
ELSIE	Sally! I think I'll call it a day...
SALLY	Righto! Don't forget the potatoes!
ELSIE	Soldier on! *(She exits)*
SALLY	I was saying... The Seamans Hostel... that's me sister... we run it together.
GEORGE	She's a good speaker...!
SALLY	Just go up this street, round the corner, and follow the tram lines...
GEORGE	Yes miss!
SALLY	A fire always burning George! A good bed, and the use of the teapot...
GEORGE	Thank you, I'll keep it in mind...
MARIA	Hey George! I not hang aroun' all day.
SALLY	The door is always open...
GEORGE	You're very kind...
SALLY	Ask, and ye shall receive...
GEORGE	If ye'll excuse me miss...

(Closes to MARIA, and they exit…)

SALLY   The tram lines George! Don't forget, follow the
                     tram lines…

                     *(Alone. Collects the posters… To audience… or the
                     remaining lounger…)*

SALLY   Jesus saves! Every Wednesday! The Gardiners
                     Hall! No collection.

                     (Exits)

                     ● ● ● ●

                     THE SEAMANS HOSTEL

                     *(Dining room. Two seamen sit and peel potatoes and
                     onions)*

1ST SEAMAN   Angels! That's what they are angels!

2ND SEAMAN   Wi' tongues o' flame.

1ST SEAMAN   Go the the Shippin' Federation and say, "present
                     address, Seamans Mission, Duke Street…"
                     "Oh", they say, "The sisters".
                     Straightaway, ye get respect.

2ND SEAMAN   Sorted it out did she?

1ST SEAMAN   Oh aye! She sorted it out alright.

                     (Enter SALLY, to peg up washing…)

SALLY   Mr Watson, Mr Mackay! You getting on with
                     those vegetables?

1ST SEAMAN   Oh Miss Sally, just telling Mr Mackay how yor
                     Elsie sorted it out…

SALLY   Sorted it out?

1ST SEAMAN   About me parrot…

                     107

SALLY	Oh your parrot…
2ND SEAMAN	Sin before God.
1ST SEAMAN	It was…

(SALLY passing MACKAY cuffs him lightly…)

SALLY	You should scrub them, not peel them. *(Exits)*
2ND SEAMAN	So what happened?
1ST SEAMAN	The' said, "It's only a parrot, and the Company rule is, no pets allowed on board".
2ND SEAMAN	What did Elsie say?
1ST SEAMAN	"A parrot's a parrot, an' he wants his two quid".
2ND SEAMAN	That what ye paid?
1ST SEAMAN	What I telled 'em… Anyhow it's not the money. A'd got attached ti that bird…
2ND SEAMAN	Good bird was it?
1ST SEAMAN	African gray… lovely bird! Just come off watch y'see. Gettin' me head down. The bo'son come shakin' us, "Get back on deck Harry, get on deck now!" Gets on deck, an' there the wicked bastard was, grinnin' all over his face… An' there was me parrot, mid-Atlantic, floatin' away on a crate…
2ND SEAMAN	Some skippers are evil Harry.
1ST SEAMAN	*(The onions are making him sniff…)* Like A say, not the money man! A loved that bird. Really loved…
2ND SEAMAN	Aye! But Elsie sorted it out?
1ST SEAMAN	Oh aye! A got me two quid…

(Enter ELSIE)

ELSIE   Mr Mackay, I've sent a letter to your Union, but I need more detail...

2ND SEAMAN   I'll give ye the facts Miss Elsie...

ELSIE   *(Note book and pen)* Come here!

(2nd Seaman dries his hands, and closes)

ELSIE   Let's see! Steamship 'Sea Rambler', Out of Dakar, Sierra Leone, May 6th. Right? You claim that on the previous morning, the skipper took in river water to avoid paying for fresh.

2ND SEAMAN   The' do it all the time Miss Elsie.

ELSIE   Was it not just for the boilers?

2ND SEAMAN   Filled the drinking tanks.

(SALLY re-enters, and puts the veg into the boiler with 1st seaman, WATSON)

ELSIE   And seven men died, before you reached Las Palmas?

2ND SEAMAN   Act of God is what they said...

ELSIE   There must have been an inquest?

2ND SEAMAN   Typhoid is what it was...

ELSIE   You were brought home as a distressed British seaman... Aug 14... but you say the British Consul impounded your discharge book? You shouldn't have allowed that Mr Mackay...

2ND SEAMAN   I've a letter from him.

ELSIE   Where's that?

2ND SEAMAN   Somewhere's in me kit.

ELSIE	When you've had the broth, go and look right! Now let's see...

(Light up 1st Seaman & SALLY)

1ST SEAMAN	Remarkable power of a woman that sister of yours...
SALLY	You'll not forget Harry...
1ST SEAMAN	What?
SALLY	The Gardiners Hall. The Gospel meeting.
1ST SEAMAN	Oh that's right Miss Sally.
SALLY	Well?
1ST SEAMAN	'Man does not live by bread alone...'
SALLY	Well done Harry. You are making progress.
1ST SEAMAN	Will there be cocoa?
SALLY	Just you be there...
1ST SEAMAN	I will... I will!

(Enter GEORGE PEARSON. Four weeks of living rough have altered him. Unshaven, disheveled... 1st SEAMAN draws the attention of the others to the arrival...)

GEORGE	Ye said, "The door would be open".
SALLY	Come in... come in!
GEORGE	"Ask, and you shall receive", that's what ye said, wasn't it?
SALLY	Please come by the fire...
1ST SEAMAN	Aye! Come in lad...
GEORGE	I don't want charity... Ye understand.

110

SALLY	Please, come and sit down...
2ND SEAMAN	Ye look all in lad.
1ST SEAMAN	Sit yourself, before ye fall...
GEORGE	Wait, I got somethin' here...

(He brings out the brass telescope from his kit bag)

This here is very old. Bound brass! Was give me by my father, who got it off his father 'long time back...

(Sways)

SALLY	Really, you should sit down...
GEORGE	Got ti be worth a bob or two. I'd say. Should cover me, 'til I get me bearin'...

(They close around and support him)

1ST SEAMAN	Steady on matey!
2ND SEAMAN	Easy mister...
SALLY	Take him thro'...

(They pass ELSIE on their way to the back room...)

ELSIE	So, what is it this time Harry. A few repairs, and back to sea?
1ST SEAMAN	I'd say dry-dock Miss, and a major refit.
ELSIE	Right then! Let's have the kettle on...

(They exit)

• • • •

THE GARDINERS HALL GOSPEL MEETING...

(Hymn 'Just As I Am'. SALLY plays a small organ, and sings first and last verse. The seamen stand and sing for their supper. Enter GEORGE. Scrubbed and shaved, and restored. To take his place with the others. At the end of the hymn they sit. SALLY resumes her ministry)

SALLY Praise be to our Heavenly Father for our brother who is come into fellowship, and the loving heart of Jesus!

(She smiles at GEORGE. The two seaman encourage him to stand. They are keeping him right in a slightly irreverent way...)

SALLY Tell us George, you were slandered and cast out...

1ST SEAMAN *(Prompting from behind)* Yes!

GEORGE Er... yes!

SALLY And looked for human aid, and there was none?

GEORGE Yes!

SALLY Near to death, and surrounded by wickedness?

GEORGE On every side!

SALLY And the lips that uttered lies, and the flames that burnt, and the teeth that devoured...?

GEORGE *(Getting into the swing)* Everywhere!

SALLY And George, did you send up a prayer, and beg for rescue?

GEORGE I cried out... *(Cued from behind)* "Lord thou art my Father... "

SALLY   Remembering the mercy of God, and those who patiently trust?

GEORGE   'Do not desert me in time of trouble'.

SALLY   And have you been answered George?

GEORGE   I have!

SALLY   Praise thee God, and Saviour, for the fulness of thy mercy. Praise thee forever!

ALL   Amen!

               (SALLY opens her bible. GEORGE sits)

1ST SEAMAN   What's happenin' about the cocoa?

2ND SEAMAN   Said nowt about cocoa.

SALLY   Ecclesiasticus 51... 13.

1ST SEAMAN   You said, 'Cocoa...'

2ND SEAMAN   Said nowt o' the sort!

SALLY   When I was young, before I set out on my travels, I asked for wisdom in my prayers...

1ST SEAMAN   Definitely said, 'Cocoa!'

2ND SEAMAN   Give it a rest...

SALLY   In the forecourt of the sanctuary, I laid claim to her. From the first blossoming to the ripening of the grape, she has been the delight of my heart. My steps have followed her without swerving...

1ST SEAMAN   Were ye just lyin' about the cocoa?

SALLY   Come to me you who need instruction, and lodge in my house of learning.

2ND SEAMAN   Norra sign o' cocoa!

1ST SEAMAN	What A' sayin'!
SALLY	Why do you admit to a lack of these things, yet leave your great thirst unslaked? Let us pray...

(Closing her eyes SALLY prays silently...)

(GEORGE turns to whisper to the others...)

GEORGE	Cocoa's off then, is it?

• • • •

PURDY's OFFICE

ELSIE	I'll not beat about the bush Mr Purdy! I have been to the offices of the Board of Trade. I have made myself familiar with the Inspectorate!
PURDY	Look miss er...
ELSIE	I have read the provisions of the Merchant Navy Shipping Act 1926, Safety Regulations, Section seven, paragraph twelve to thirty seven.
PURDY	Er!
ELSIE	At sea, or docked!
PURDY	Listen...!
ELSIE	Especially concerning the level of water in bilges, and the regular inspection of bilge pumps, provision of which...
PURDY	Miss er...
ELSIE	I am not one of your ignorant sailors Mr Purdy...
PURDY	Pearson! Pearson you said...
ELSIE	George Pearson!

PURDY   George Pearson! Seems familiar, Does it seem familiar to you Mr eh...?

THOMPSON   Yes Mr Purdy, I think I remember...

ELSIE   I should think you jolly well might! It being less than three months since you put him out of work, after six years of umblemished service...

PURDY   Umblemished?

ELSIE   Unless you have documented evidence to the contrary. And I suggest you put a memo into the North-East Coast Fishing Vessel Owners Association.

PURDY   A memo!...

ELSIE   Civil Law Mr Purdy.

PURDY   Now look here my good woman...

ELSIE   A good woman I am, but not yours Mr Purdy, or anyone else's for that matter...

PURDY   If you...

ELSIE   If you are not aware that it is an offence under a statute of Civil Law to proscribe a citizen of this country by indenture with an association of companies, and or individuals for the purpose of preventing that citizen from securing employment, than I suggest you seek out a good solicitor.

PURDY   Miss er... just tell me one thing!
               What exactly is your interest in this George Pearson?

ELSIE   He is a man... who has suffered an injustice...

               (She exits... imperiously)

               (Thompson politely moves to the door and opens it to allow her exit... he closes the door)

115

PURDY   Thompson!

THOMPSON   Sir?

PURDY   Get out!

• • • •

THE SHORE BY TYNEMOUTH PIER.

(SALLY and GEORGE scramble over the rocks. Off stage the sound of surf)

SALLY   Give us your hand George, C'mon! There!

(They pause for breath)

SALLY   It's so lovely here! The wind, the spray... but
             you'll be used to that.
             When we were small, our dad would bring us
             climbing over these rocks, when the seas were
             running in from the North-East, and the great
             waves came bursting over the piers.
             "Behold the power of God!"
             I used to cling to him, terrified.
             "Granite!" he'd say, "Tynemouth Pier is built of
             Aberdeen granite."
             But the ocean is forever isn't it?
             C'mon George, let's climb higher up.

             *(They scramble to a higher point. GEORGE assisting
             SALLY comes into bodily contact. GEORGE is
             apologetic)*

SALLY   It's alright George! In the sight of the Lord, it is
             perfectly alright for a gentleman to support a
             lady when she is stepping over seaweed, and
             rock pools.

             *(She holds out her hands. GEORGE takes it. Then dis-
             engages, and moves...)*

SALLY   You've been married, haven't you George?
             If you'd rather not talk about it!

116

GEORGE   She was from Aberdeen, but she wasn't made of strong stuff.
              We had a room down Tyne Street. Pulmonary Tuberculosis! Is what it said on the certificate. Should never have brought her ti this town…
              Anyhow! That's what I have left. A death certificate, and a photograph took afore we married… The' took all her things y'see. Clothes, bits an' pieces, personal stuff… ti the Scaffold Hill hospital for fumigatin'…
              Don' know why? Did'n have a fever… A never bothered goin' back ti fetch them. Thirty two she was…

SALLY   Sorry!

GEORGE   It's alright. It's past history. We'd no family!

SALLY   There a lot of Pearsons in Shields?

GEORGE   Aye. Wi seem ti be widespread, but we've no claim ti each other…
              But what about yourself? You, and your sister… such opposites!

SALLY   Well, we've lived together since our parents died. It's true we have different ways of looking at things, but what we believe comes from the same beginning…
              We are very close, in heart, and mind.

GEORGE   She's good crack mind. Makes you think a bit does yor Elsie. A mean once she gets started… Gets you right worked up.
              But dialectical materialism? What in a herrin's heed does that mean?

● ● ● ●

THE LABOUR COLLEGE. NORTH SHIELDS.

(The two seamen sit bored but patient. They are joined by GEORGE)

ELSIE   A word invented by Aristotle to describe the art

117

of conversation.
Thesis, and anti-thesis.
But comrades! What Marx is really saying,
Lay claim to the future...
Never look back regretfully.

(GEORGE claps politely)

ELSIE   There is nothing mysterious or uncertain in
               progress.
               It is governed by simple laws, and logic...
               Above all understand yourselves.
               Understand the relationship of the individual
               to the social conditions that shape our destiny.

               (The SEAMEN yawn, and look distractedly around)

ELSIE   Do not dread what is to come...
               Comrades, history is in your hands.

               *(GEORGE applauds vigorously. ELSIE is delighted
               she has such a fervent supporter)*

ELSIE   Recast the mould. That is what Marx is saying
               to you.
               Arise ye starvellings from your slumber...
               Reason in revolt now thunders.
               The Inter-nation-ale unites the human race...

               (GEORGE is on his feet clapping wildly)

ELSIE   Thank you George.

               (She unfurls the red flag)

ELSIE   Take the banner!

               (GEORGE self consciously holds it)

ELSIE   And comrades, come rally!
               And the last fight let us face.
               But before we take our meeting onto the street...

               *(She brings from behind the platform a jug and
               mugs)*

ELSIE   Some refreshment!

                 (She pours)

ELSIE   Is that everyone?

                 (She takes the jug away)

GEORGE   That's the dif'rence!
                 Wi' Karl Marx, there's cocoa!

                 (The SEAMEN agree)

●　●　●　●

EXT. THE STREET.

(Outside PURDY's office. Off stage an altercation. SPANISH MARIA is ejected. A tirade of Spanish abuse.)

MARIA   Don' you tell me 'be about my business' I know
                 my business.
                 Me, I wouldn't dirty me feet on your carpet... an'
                 another thing, if I was comin' to seek men, this be
                 the lasta bloody place. You notta men, you pile a
                 shit...ok.

                 (SALLY approaches)

MARIA   Hey miss! you goin' in there, well you watch
                 yourself alright! They don' know how to treat a
                 lady...

                 (MARIA staggers off. Exits)

MARIA   Men! Better to sell fish...

●　●　●　●

INT. PURDY's OFFICE.

(THOMPSON shows in SALLY)

PURDY   Sorry about that, Miss er...

THOMPSON	Robson!
PURDY	Yes! Have a chair. Thompson!
	(THOMPSON assists SALLY to a chair)
PURDY	I was reading Priestly in the 'Sunday Journal'. First time he ever saw a woman drunk on a public street... Tyneside! Sad reflection!
SALLY	Sad reflection on Mr Priestly to be so occupied... You got my letter Mr Purdy?
PURDY	*(Blankly)* Letter? Yes, er Thompson, the letter!
	(THOMPSON gropes thro' a file)
SALLY	It would be doing the Lord's work.
	(THOMPSON fumbles the letter over to PURDY)
PURDY	Yes! *(Hurriedly perusing it obviously for the first time)*
SALLY	Just the small haddocks! Is it 'tidds' you call them? Well, rather than they should go to the Fish Meal Factory, or be dumped at sea.
PURDY	Miss er...
SALLY	Which is after all throwing His bounty back into the face of God. A terrible, and shameful act, as you a good church...
PURDY	Chapel!
SALLY	Will readily appreciate.
PURDY	Of course!
SALLY	Now let us see... If there is a surplus to requirement on the market, of any particular specie, no matter how lowly... Just to set aside one or two boxes for a free...

120

PURDY   Free!

SALLY   Distribution to the unemployed, poor, and needy families of the town.

PURDY   But...

SALLY   Which would be doing God's work, and for which you would be blessed.

PURDY   The Traders...

SALLY   Ah the Traders, simple, decent, hard working, and charitable men. Close to the life of Jesus in their work, and deeds, I so admire them.

PURDY   Miss... they wouldn't...

SALLY   Mind!

PURDY   Stand for it!

SALLY   Cast thy bread upon the waters, Mr Purdy.
               He that hath pity upon the poor, lendeth to the Lord. Therefore I command you saying, 'Thou shalt open thine hand wide to thy brother.'

PURDY   Miss...

SALLY   For this thing the Lord Thy God shall bless thee in all thy works...

PURDY   Why are you doing this Miss er...

SALLY   Oh! for love Mr Purdy.

PURDY   Yes...

               (Thrusting THOMPSON out of the way, he personally escorts SALLY out of the office)

PURDY   How is you sister Miss Robson?

• • • •

THE SHORE BY TYNEMOUTH PIER.

(GEORGE and ELSIE clamber over the rocks. Off stage the sound of surf)

ELSIE   C'mon George, up here! Give 's your hand...
      That's it. There! Hold on!

(She links his arm... breathes the salt air deeply)

ELSIE   Wonderful isn't it?
      Our father liked bringing us here.

GEORGE To see the waves crashing over the pier...

ELSIE   That's right! How did you know?
      Very dramatic. Used to terrify our Sal. She'd
      shriek, and cling to him, begging him not to let
      go.
      Poor Sal!

GEORGE Close to her dad was she?

ELSIE   Somehow for her, he's still around.

GEORGE And for you?

ELSIE   What's all this father dependancy about? When
      a father's dead, he's dead!
      You look around, there's all kind of fathers, some
      good, some bad, but all they've got in common,
      is they come, and go...

GEORGE *(Disengages from her)*

      Havin' someone to look up to isn't it?

ELSIE   Fine! So long as he's around. But what if he gets
      sick? Leaves home! Gets fed up with the sight
      of kids... What if he dies?
      Where does it leave you? What is it going to do
      to your self-reliance? No! This whole beneficent
      Father thing has got out of hand.

GEORGE   Feel as if I should be going back to mine... but I don't know where I left him... Like a long time ago...

ELSIE   George! Too much of a cop out. Even fathers have got fathers.
I blame Abraham. And that's another thing... Sacrificing their off spring, they're all into that...

GEORGE   You sayin' fathers is unnecessary?

ELSIE   You are standing on a very slippery rock there George. Better let me hang on to you...

(She takes hold of him again...)

GEORGE   So what about mothers?

ELSIE   Worse again! You're not looking for one are you George?
No! Where I part company from Sally is over the 'Which art in heaven', our father...
You want more responsibility from a man than that.
Reminds me! Tomorrow night!
Sally and I have to chair this joint Trades Council/Evangelical Church Committee...
We'll be out late...
You look after the Mission for us George.

GEORGE   Sure.

ELSIE   See that everything is kept in order...
Come on! We better move, the tides coming in...

(They walk off)

ELSIE   Could have some good news from the Trawler Owners Association.
I think you could be getting your job back...

• • • •

THE SEAMAN's HOSTEL.

(A darkened front room. Spanish MARIA, and the two SEAMEN enter)

2ND SEAMAN	C'mon. It'll be alright!
MARIA	You sure?
2ND SEAMAN	Didn' I tell you. They's away to a meetin'. George is in charge.

(They stumble over chairs)

MARIA	I don' know…
1ST SEAMAN	Light the gas…
2ND SEAMAN	You got a match?
1ST SEAMAN	Maria! You gorra match?
MARIA	I gorra my hands full…
2ND SEAMAN	Herc! I gorra match…

(The sratch and splutter of a match. The gas is lit. MARIA is carrying bags of food and drink. They lay it out on the table. GEORGE enters… Disapproval…)

MARIA	Hello George!
2ND SEAMAN	Just a little drink George. That's not so bad eh?
MARIA	How are you George? Long time no see.

(2ND SEAMAN fishes out a bottle of spirit)

2ND SEAMAN	Kinda drink is this then?
MARIA	Hey! That's a good drink. Come off a Greek ship.
2ND SEAMAN	Smells like it come off a Greek ship.

1ST SEAMAN	Hey you are a Spanish marvel Maria.
	(They laugh, but GEORGE is worried)
MARIA	Everybody say Spanish Maria, but I a Portageese, ' know that's truth.
	(The men are investigating the bag)
2ND SEAMAN	What's the grub then?
MARIA	What you like eh! It's a savaloy, a pease puddin', a pickle onion. Hey George, why you lookin' sad? Gonna be a party ain't it? Gedda good time goin'... you OK George?
GEORGE	I'm alright!
MARIA	Look, I get special for you. Hey you two get outa there, let me in.
	(Pushes the TWO SEAMEN off the bag. Takes out a pork sandwich)
MARIA	Look! One juicy pork sandwich.
	(Advances on GEORGE)
MARIA	Dippa the bun in the gravy. Bit o' cracklin', bit o' mustard... Eh!
	(Seductively offers it to his mouth)
MARIA	All for you George!
	(GEORGE Hesitates... then bites. The TWO SEAMEN cheer. GEORGE has accepted the party)
1ST SEAMAN	Hcy Pork butcher good to you Maria?
MARIA	You got it wrong way round. It's a Maria is good to the pork butcher.
	(They relieve the tension with laughter)

1ST SEAMAN	C'mon get the cups.
2ND SEAMAN	You know where they are, you gett 'm.
1ST SEAMAN	OK. I gett 'm. You get the tops off.
2ND SEAMAN	Right. I get the tops off.
	(1ST SEAMAN troops off to the kitchen)
MARIA	You sure those two sisters don' come back catchin' us all of a sudden?
2ND SEAMAN	No, we got plenty time. They won't be back…
MARIA	That right George?
GEORGE	That's right. Yeh!
MARIA	The holy one I don' mind. But the other one, she worry me… She can talk plenty.
GEORGE	She's alright. She's good to poor people.
MARIA	She good to you George? You a poor people.
GEORGE	Done a lot for all us. I tell you.
MARIA	I hear she get your job back. That right?
GEORGE	We owe them a lot.
MARIA	But George! Poor people got to have a birra fun… eh!
GEORGE	They are alright…
MARIA	*(Closes to him)* Hey George, you don' do it to her do you?
GEORGE	Lay off Maria…
MARIA	C'mon, I only joke…

               (1ST SEAMAN returns from kitchen. They pour the drinks. Imbibe freely. Toasting each other…)

MARIA   Here's to you George!

SEAMEN
(Together)   Yeh! C'mon! Drink up! Get it down! Cats away!

1ST SEAMAN   It's OK Sister Sally, tonight we have a drink. Tomorrow we all go your Gospel meeting…

               (Produces his concertina. Playing the hymn 'Just as I am'. 2ND SEAMAN placing his hands together in mock prayer, sing a parody…)

2ND SEAMAN   Just as I am, without one flea,
If I stay here, how long will it be,
For a bed, an' grub, an' a cup o' tea,
O' Jesus, I'll come to thee…

1ST SEAMAN   C'mon! Why aye! Fill 'm up George!
Altogether!
Just as we are, without…

• • • •

THE MEETING. TRADES COUNCIL/CHURCH UNION

ELSIE   Elsie Robson, National Union of Unemployed Workers.
Drawing the committee's attention to the first item on the agenda. The provision of unsold fish to poor, and needy families…
I call upon my sister to outline the problems.

SALLY   Sally Robson, Independant Church Union.
Following our approach to the Trawler Owners, and Wholesale Fish Merchants, it was provisonally arranged that some boxes of fish be put to one side from unsold stocks.
On Thursday last week…

ELSIE   Thursday was it?

SALLY	Out of three hundred and seventy five hundred weight of withdrawn fish.
ELSIE	That is over 19, very nearly 20 ton of fish comrades!
SALLY	Withdrawn...
ELSIE	Withdrawn...
SALLY	That is fish designated for pulping into fertiliser... Six were put to oneside for public disposal.
ELISE	*(High indignation)* Six!
SALLY	I'm afraid what followed could only be described as unfortunate.
ELSIE	I heard it was a bloody shambles...
SALLY	There were some complaints...
ELSIE	Absolute bloody shambles!
SALLY	With hindsight.
ELSIE	Scrambling... fighting!
SALLY	Things might have been better...
ELSIE	People need to be organised...
SALLY	We are all genuinely concerned Elsie!
ELSIE	Genuine needy couldn't get a look in.
SALLY	Sheep without a shepherd perhaps.
ELSIE	I heard there were women there in fur coats.
SALLY	One lady was wearing a fur coat...
ELSIE	What was she doing with free fish?

SALLY   I think she was making sure it was fresh.

ELSIE   Huh!

SALLY   The six boxes were piled up to be distributed...
               progressively...

ELSIE   Tipped over, and rummaged is what I heard...

SALLY   Yes, well! The outcome is, unfortunately! The
               trawler owners under pressure from the
               merchants, have withdrawn the concession.

ELSIE   A serious setback...

SALLY   My friends, the parable of the feeding of the five
               thousand...

ELSIE   Oh that...

SALLY   Elsie please!

ELSIE   You can see what must have happened there.
               Those two fishes, and five loaves have been
               meant for a dozen people, and they got wind of
               it in Whitley Bay...

SALLY   That is not in good taste Elsie...

ELSIE   Jesus, look at the fur coats.

SALLY   Elsie!

ELSIE   We are not dealing in parables or miracles
               Sally... this is 1930...

SALLY   I'm afraid we are dealing with the will of God
               Elsie...

ELSIE   The will of God we can cope with... It is the
               wilfulness of people that defeats us.

● ● ● ●

THE HOSTEL DINING ROOM.

*(The party in full swing. 1ST SEAMAN concertina.
2ND SEAMAN sings. GEORGE & MARIA tipsy.
Arm in arm, applaud)*

2ND SEAMAN   When you are stony broke
And you haven't got a smoke,
And you want a couple o' shiners,
Take my tip,
And take a trip,
On one of the cowshit liners.

They leave Newcastle Quay,
An' you work yor passage free,
Day, and night,
Shovellin' shite,
On one of the Cow shit liners.

Even if you got f... all,
You will get to Montreal,
An' you'll love the smell o' the diner,

Custard an' plums,
From the moo cow bums,
On one of the cow shit liners.

1ST SEAMAN   That's what you should do George, sign on the deep sea, get away from the fishin'...

GEORGE   Couldn't leave Shields.

1ST SEAMAN   Anybody can leave Shields. I stood on the rail Alexandria, this box come floating past, on the side was written... 'Must not leave North Shields Fish Quay'. If a box can get out George...

2ND SEAMAN   Aye! Only way you can get out in a fuckin' box...

MARIA   Watcha yor tongue...

2ND SEAMAN   'Scuse me Maria!

GEORGE

I once done an Iceland trip, far enough for me.
Y' know I never see an iceberg before.
This Grimsby scrob, he says ti me. "Look Geordie! Y'see that iceborg."
Cos they has this funny way o' talkin'...

(Produces his telescope and drunkenly surveys)

GEORGE

Y' see that iceborg. There's penguins on that.
Wasn't penguins man! Was only bloody seagulls...
Was 'e think I was... stupid?

2ND SEAMAN

Ye don' want the deep sea George, No! I tell you what the sea is. You listenin'?

GEORGE

Wassat?

2ND SEAMAN

The sea! It's the biggest cemetery in the world.

MARIA

Don' give us that misery talk...

1ST SEAMAN

C'mon man! Lay off!

2ND SEAMAN

Listen, I tell ye. I go back to sea, 'cos I don' wanna spend a year dying.
I wanna go sudden. Y' know Maria, they stitch you up in a canvas bag.

MARIA

Sharrap! I don' wanna hear!

1ST SEAMAN

Yeh! Leave it be man! Have a drink.

2ND SEAMAN

I tell ye. Y' sick, y' die, y' get stitched up is a canvas bag. Didn' I see seven of me mates go like that?

1ST SEAMAN

Aw fer cris' sake...

2ND SEAMAN

An' the last stitch Maria, they put it thro' yor nose...

1ST SEAMAN

C'mon Maria, give 's a song...

MARIA

Naw he make me feel miserable. I sing miserable.

131

GEORGE	Then this Grimsby scrob he says, 'There's polar bears on them iceborgs. Ye gotta watch out. 'Cos at night, if the ship dunches the iceborg, the polar bears jumps onto the deck.' Eh! Worra ye think o' that...?
1ST SEAMAN	I don' wanna think o' that. I want Maria ti sing a song... C'mon Maria...
GEORGE	Yeh C'mon Maria...
MARIA	You want I should sing for you George?
GEORGE	'Course you sing! Sing that Spanish song.
MARIA	OK OK. I sing for you George... *(1ST SEAMAN accompanies on the concertina. Secuctively she gyrates before GEORGE)* Ate Mahia, Tu de Bore Qui amore. Y' son muton amo son ficare, Termine yo' mainor i' amore. Y' son muton amo son ficare...
ALL	*(They chorus together)* La. La. La... etc. *(MARIA takes up GEORGE, and dances with him. Encourages the 2ND SEAMAN out of his melancholy. Ends with a passionate embrace of GEORGE while the other two look on approvingly)*

• • • •

THE STREET.

(ELSIE & SALLY are walking back from the meeting)

SALLY	You had no right to alter the agenda Elsie.
ELSIE	All I did was bring it forward...
SALLY	The soup kitchen was on the agenda.
ELSIE	So was the deputation to the Town Clerk.

SALLY	It's what we agreed...
ELSIE	Then it's good news for all sinners.
SALLY	Man does not...
ELSIE	Live by bread alone... I know Sally, I know... They live in this wilderness. We have to lead them out.
SALLY	Then how better than with the smell of hot food...
ELSIE	Sally! What have we become? Politics, and religion... the Bisto kids! We need a banner, and a drum.
SALLY	We need a bible, and a pan of broth.
ELSIE	Do we march, or peel potatoes?
SALLY	We are satisfying hungers, spiritual and temporal...
ELSIE	I want us to lift up our heads, and cry freedom. Not bow them down to say grace...
SALLY	Bible and broth!
ELSIE	Banner and drum.
SALLY	Bible and broth.
ELSIE	Sally!... are you not sick of soup?

• • • •

THE PARTY.

(It has subsided into stupor. MARIA is cradled in GEORGE's arms. The two seamen snore peacefully)

MARIA	Hey! C'mon George, we gotta get this place a bit tidy, then I gotta go, or you in trouble 'cos ' me.

GEORGE   Mmmmm!

MARIA   George I just a poor people like you. It worries
                me I get old, and sick, an' don' wanna be buried
                by the Parish George!
                Don' let that happen to Maria eh?
                You listen?
                No! You got the drink in you. You got the peas
                puddin' in you, an' the pork sandwich, an' you
                got a woman to lie on.
                What more do a poor people want?

                (She frees herself from his embrace. Rising up)

GEORGE   Where ye goin'?

MARIA   What matter? I dunno! Maybe I walk down by
                the ferry.

GEORGE   You catchin' the ferry?

MARIA   Maybe! Maybe I jus' watch the lights of the town
                dancin' on the river.
                It's like a lot o' stars...
                Sometimes I get this crazy feelin' I could walk
                across them to the other side...

GEORGE   Maybe it's rainin'...

MARIA   Maybe, maybe! What a lot o' maybes.
                Maybes is all a poor peoples can think of sayin'...
                C'mon George!

                *(She pulls him to his feet. ELSIE and SALLY come
                quietly into the room)*

MARIA   Maybe I let you take me in a shop door, an' you
                can be a rich man for a short time...
                Then maybe we walk the river stars together...

                (She becomes aware of the sisters)

MARIA   George!

GEORGE   Yeh!

MARIA   George!

GEORGE   Mmmm!

MARIA   The polar bears is on deck!

             (GEORGE becomes aware of the sisters)

GEORGE   Oh' Cris'... I... er... look! We soon get this put
             right... I'm sorry... I...

             (Knocking the SEAMEN awake)

GEORGE   C'mon ye lugs, get up, an' get this place cleaned
             up. D'ye hear?

             *(Roused, the SEAMEN are deferential to the sisters,
             and stumble into action, clearing up the bottles,
             cups, paper. 1ST SEAMAN takes a sweeping brush
             to the floor)*

MARIA   I sorry about this.

GEORGE   Yeh! What time is it?

1ST SEAMAN   We jus' have a little drink, an' a bite, y' know
             Elsie... Yeh! that's it, but we get everythin'
             cleared up quick...

GEORGE   Look, it's all my fault...

1ST SEAMAN   No! it's not his fault, we all y' know...

2ND SEAMAN   Yeh! that's right, we all...

             (They clink and fumble the bottles into a bag)

MARIA   Gimme, I take them...

GEORGE   We don' mean no disrespect...

1ST SEAMAN   No, not at all, no disrespect.

2ND SEAMAN   Certainly not, no disrespect at all. But we get it
             ship shape, and Bristol fashion.

1ST SEAMAN	That's right! C'mon bo'sun, you get under there…
ELSIE	I think, first thing in the morning we can talk this over.
1ST SEAMAN	Yes, yor right Elsie! She's right yeh!. Better to talk about it in the morning.
2ND SEAMAN	I go along with that… yeh!
MARIA	I… er… very sorry! I can't tell you.
ELSIE	Maybe, if you just left us now.
MARIA	I like to clean the table, an' floor, if I can have a bucket, and cloth. I like to do that…
1ST SEAMAN	Yeh! She'd do that good Elsie. I can get the bucket for her…
ELSIE	It's alright. Just… go!
MARIA	Yes, It's right. I better do that.
	(Begins to leave)
GEORGE	Maria! Hold on! Wait for me!
MARIA	Wait for you?
GEORGE	Outside… wait for me!
MARIA	Oh George, that's not right. Not now.
GEORGE	Do as I say. Wait for me. Go on!
	(MARIA leaves. GEORGE follows her. Returns. The sisters wait impassively. GEORGE goes to the hall, comes out with his kit bag)
GEORGE	I know you feel we let you down… an' we have… I'm sorry we use your house like this. I want to say, I really appreciate all you done for me, in the time I been here.

ELSIE   Look George...

GEORGE   No! Let me say... you an' Miss Sally have been
               really good to me. Not just you look after me,
               but I'm learnin' from you.
               You made me think a lot, about everythin'.
               I don' know, I wouldn't ever have got ti know
               about things, but you showed me.
               I reckon you told it to me, so I got to hear things
               I never heard before...
               I want you to know, I really am grateful to you
               for all that...
               You must look at people like me, an' wonder...
               is it worth it?

SALLY   George... listen!

GEORGE   It's worth it, 'cos I want to be like you, y' see! Be
               the way you are...

SALLY   But George...

GEORGE   That's how I see it... I don't want to just be
               hangin' aroun' havin' things done for me. I want
               to be givin' carin' back to someone else.

ELSIE   George!

GEORGE   Don' let me lose what I'm tryin' ti say. You are
               good people, but you gotta understand, people
               like us... like me... we got lost. An' we gotta
               start off again from somewhere. That's what
               poor people have got ti do... We ain't used ti
               carin' for a lot o' people, like the whole world,
               an' that. When you get lost, you just get on with
               people you bump into...
               Maybe we got to make a start that way, carin' for
               one, then when we get better at it, carin' for two,
               or maybe three, until one day, we'll be like you,
               an' carin' about everybody...
               Anyhow, that's how I work it out...

               (*He goes across the room, picks up his kit bag*)

GEORGE

Y' see, I been preparin' myself ti sayin' this. I had the bag packed an'... well! I already signed on. I'm sailin' dawn tomorrow. It's a trawler called the 'Jeannie Stewart'... But what I don't want you to think is badly of me. I don't want you to think I walked out with bad feelin'...

ELSIE

(Picking up his telescope) You'll be needing this then.

GEORGE

I think you should keep that.

ELSIE

Wouldn't be right George. Here! It belongs to your family.

SALLY

George, you can't go off into the night. Where will you go? What will you do?

GEORGE

Oh we'll find somewhere's dry, and comfortable. An' I gotta make a start lookin' after this person I'm carin' about...
Be dawn soon, an' she likes to see the lights on the river.
Then afore I put myself aboard, I wanna get her fixed up thinking about where she's gonna be nex' week, an' maybe the week after...

SALLY

Is she a praying person George?

GEORGE

Oh! She don' think too far ahead.
Anyhow! Goodbye! An' thanks...

(He shakes hands with them awkwardly)

1ST SEAMAN

So long George...

2ND SEAMAN

So long mate...

(GEORGE leaves. They look at each other in bewilderment)

SALLY

Well!... Well!... Well!

ELSIE

Well what?

SALLY   Well don't just stand there. Somebody! Put the
bloody kettle on...

● ● ● ●

Interval

PART THREE
'A boy from Shields'

1990

George Pearson (known as Digga. Grandson of
George Pearson in Part Two)

Betty	George's mother
Andy	Her boyfriend
Linda	Her daughter
Grippa	George's pal
Ray	
Scampi Jack	
Natalie	

THE LOW NEWTON REMAND PRISON.

*(Int. Reception area. GEORGE PEARSON stripped,
is being prepared for admission. PRISON OFfiCER
with clip board gives him a hard time)*

P. OFFICER   George Pearson! 702! Back again! What for this time?

(Consults his clip board)

P. OFFICER   Assault! Robbery!

GEORGE   A was set up!

P. OFFICER   Aye 702. They all say that.

GEORGE   What's the point, talkin' ti you's...

P. OFFICER   Shut yor mouth 702, an' call me sir.

GEORGE   Why shoulda?

P. OFFICER   'Cos if you don't, I'll put you down the fuckin' block, that's why.

GEORGE   Oh ye scare me! Ye forget man, A've been here before...

P. OFFICER   Too many times son...

GEORGE   So what's it to you?

P. OFFICER   Jus' one thing 702. You help me stay in a job.
Spread! C'mon!

(Peers into his crutch)

P.OFFICER   Any complaints?

GEORGE   Yeh! The paddy wagon was freezin'!

P. OFFICER   Was freezin' sir...

(Consults the pad)

P.OFFICER   Judges remand! Crown Court! Committal Low
Newton! Social Worker, Mrs Parker.

GEORGE   She said A was gonna get community service.

P. OFFICER   Yor a joker 702. Yor in for a stretch.
(Reading) There will be an accommodation
problem on release.
Where you gonna live son?

GEORGE   Don' friggin' know... sir!

P. OFFICER   Then I'll tell ye. Low Newton, then Durham,
then Frankland High Security. In that order. All
close together so nobody's inconvenienced...

P.OFFICER   *(To the con with the sweeping brush)* Hey, you!
Loppy Lugs! You swept that same place three
times. Piss off!
(Reading) Mother does not want him home
anymore...
Ah!
Over there!

*(Moves GEORGE to the wall where he faces a
window)*

GEORGE   The bitch! Bloody cow! She cared nowt about me!
         But A don' give a shit. The rotten hoo-a!

P. OFFICER   'C' Wing... rule 43...

         (The con with the sweeping brush exchanges a glance with the PRISON OFFICER)

GEORGE   Friggin' cow!

Mix   *(His face is seen from the outside of the window. He remembers. The window becomes the window of his home. He is looking into the lane. His mother BETTY comes into the lane engaged in an argument with a seaman)*

• • • •

EXT. DAY. REAR OF BETTY's HOUSE.

         (ANDREW & BETTY embrace. Conscious of being overlooked, BETTY shrugs him off)

BETTY   No! Andy! No! Please! 'Course A love ye man! No! Don't!
         Look, A'll be seein' ye.

ANDY   Is that it then? Fer Cris' sake!

BETTY   Sssh man! Pack it in!

ANDY   Naw! C'mon Betty, what ye givin' us?

BETTY   I'll be sure ti get some time off.

ANDY   No on aboot ye workin'...
         Betty, look! When ye gonna make a decision?

BETTY   Y' know how it is?

ANDY   That's the trouble... A don't.

BETTY   It's tellin' them...

ANDY   Fer Cris' sake. They're no children. Got ti find oot sometime...

BETTY   Keep ye gob down man! Ye'll have everybody nebbin'...

ANDY   At nineteen Betty! I'd been ti sea fer three years...

BETTY   Misses his da! That's been the thing really...

ANDY   What ye talkin' aboot?

BETTY   Was close to him. A think in a way he blames me...

ANDY   Some bloody da! Ye've no clapped eyes on him fer six years...
Can ye's remember what he looked like?

BETTY   Oh aye! Wi can remember.

ANDY   Aw shite!

BETTY   Andy!

ANDY   S'marrer? The neighbours! Oh aye! The folks o' Shields. Witty, watterin' on!
What ye let them bother ye for?
They're no unique:
Betty, I'm frae Port Seton. The' scrub the bloody pavements ootside thor front doors...

      (He takes hold of her again)

ANDY   Betty! A get on well wi' young'ens. Just invite me in...

BETTY   He gets up in the mornin' an' ye never know how ye have him. Sometimes he never speaks...

ANDY   We're makin' problems fer oorsels.

Mix   *(Light up. Living room interior. Tele is showing The Flintstones. LINDA comes in and settles down on*

> *the floor to watch. GEORGE returns from the window and watches the tele thro' a brass telescope)*

BETTY *(V.O)*   Linda's alright!

ANDY *(V.O)*   What chance have we had ti get tigether?

BETTY *(V.O)*   But it's George! I'm really worried. He's been in that much bother.

ANDY *(V.O)*   Maybe I can talk to him Betty! I'm just flesh, an' blood mesel'.

BETTY *(V.O)*   Oh well, C'mon!

• • • •

INT. THE LIVING ROOM...

(The Flintsones... The living room door opens, BETTY pops her head round)

BETTY   Hello luv!

LINDA   Hi Mam!

BETTY   What ye's watchin'?

LINDA   Flintstones...

BETTY   Good is it?

LINDA   Alright...

BETTY   Look who's here! Di ye remember Andrew? Come on in Andrew!

(They both fully enter the room)

ANDY   Hello there! Ye's a'right?

(LINDA spares him a glance out of curiousity. GEORGE goes on watching the tele...)

LINDA   Did ye get the tomato sauce?

BETTY	Oh A knew there was somethin'.
LINDA	Aw Ma.
BETTY	Can gerrit after, up at the Paki's. Be no bother.
ANDY	Tie a knot in yor leg eh?
BETTY	Y'what?
ANDY	So's ye'll not...
LINDA	Always forgettin'...
BETTY	Linda, A've been on me feet all day snappin' prawns.
ANDY	Aw! That's mind bendin'. What size was the'?
BETTY	Beetles! Scampi Jack buys nowt else. Look Linda! Why don't ye put the kettle on. We'll have a cup o' coffee eh! Fancy a cup o' coffee Andrew? Linda! Linda I'm askin' ye.
LINDA	Watchin' this...
BETTY	Could still put the kettle on.
	(No response)
BETTY	Alright, I'll put it on meself. Sit down man Andrew. Take yor coat off.
	(She goes into the kitchen. ANDY takes stock of the room. GEORGE ignores him. LINDA glued to the tele)
BETTY *(V.O)*	Andrew is on that big new seine net boat, just landed this mornin'... What's it called...?
ANDY	The 'Shemara'...
BETTY *(V.O)*	Aye, the 'Shemara'

145

(Pops her head back round the door)

BETTY   What was it Andrew? Seven hundred boxes for four days...

(Goes back)

ANDY   Oh aye! She's got the lot has that boat.
Built in Scotland eh! Talkin' near enuff a million.

BETTY *(V.O)*   Pounds?

ANDY   Oh aye! She's got everythin'...

LINDA   *(Shouting thro' to her mother)* What about the fish fingers?

BETTY *(V.O)*   What about the fish fingers?

LINDA   Did ye get them?

(BETTY returns)

BETTY   Will ye listen to her. Fish bloody fingers. A fisherman's daughter, an' she's goin' on about fish fingers.

(Goes back into the kitchen)

ANDY   Mark 52 Decca Navigation! Atlas colour sounder! Scanners! Auto-pilot.
She's a bloody electronic marvel. You name it! It's no givin' the fish a chance. Like printin' money...
'Course there's nae the fish, or the market doon here. We'll be awa' back tae Peterheed tun o' the month.

BETTY *(V.O)*   Nowt like that in Shields eh George?

ANDY   Aye gud boat the 'Shemara'. Gud skipper is Duggie Moodie. It's the way it is in Scotland. The' keep it in the family.
He's four sons wi' four boats, an' the wives do the settlin's.

They'll no get caught up wi' the Companies...
Shields... huh! What the' deein' tae it?
It's fallin' apart. Everytime wi' put in there seems less of it...
Them flats where ye lived...

BETTY *(V.O)* King's Court. They've gone...

ANDY Aye A remember...

BETTY *(V.O)* Pulled them down. Only been up fifteen year. Was like livin' in Durham jail. Whoever built them, that's where the' want lockin' up.

ANDY An' that fish quay! It's a joke!
Pre-pack city! *(Laughs)*
No a decent merchant on it. All little shops.
But if ye want a blacksmith, a rigger or an engineer... nae chance...
'Maybe this afternoon, maybe timorrow mornin'.
An' ice! A cud tell ye! It's the dearest ice on the East coast, an' ye've tae put aboard yorsel'...

(LINDA furious at being unable to listen to the tele. Goes to join her mother in the kitchen)

ANDY Mind! A can remember Shields in its better days. Irvins, an' Purdys!
Aye old George Purdy! They've gone all tigether haven't they?
All them trawlers, an' fact'ry freeezers... all gone... what a mess...
Tae me, Shields is finished...

(Mix to the kitchen)

LINDA Is he stoppin'?

BETTY Linda don't start.

LINDA Well, is 'e?

BETTY A don't know...

LINDA	A hate that little bedroom, it's freezin'.
BETTY	Once! A only once ever asked ye.
LINDA	More than once. What about…
BETTY	Linda, don't winge…
LINDA	So borin'! Rabbitin' on. Cannit watch the tele.
BETTY	Give us a hand wi' this coffee.
LINDA	Hate coffee.
BETTY	Well don't bloody have any. Nobody is forcin' ye.
LINDA	When wi havin' our dinner?
BETTY	A've jus' come in fer God's sake.
LINDA	A'm hungry.
BETTY	Yor never anythin' else.
LINDA	Starvin'…
BETTY	Well get away down ti the chippy.
LINDA	Need some money…
BETTY	Where's that fifty pence A give ye.
LINDA	Fifty pence! What's that?
BETTY	Where's me purse…
	(Hunts for her purse)
LINDA	A don't like sleepin' on me own Mam.
BETTY	Here! There's a pund… Bugga off!

(*LINDA exits. BETTY re-enters the living room with the coffees*)

BETTY   Di ye take sugar Andrew? A couldn't remember.

ANDY   A was just sayin' the boats here is all scratchin'. Prawns!

BETTY   Don' talk ti me about prawns.

ANDY   Shields has a coupla gud boats, the 'Neilson', the 'Lindisfarne', but that's it...

BETTY   Finger nails is droppin' off...

ANDY   Prawns! It's no fishin'. Dredgin' friggin' mud. Cris' gi' me the clear water. Prawns is shite. No way! It's different fishin' up in Peterheed.

BETTY   Is that strong enough for ye?

ANDY   A was jus' sayin' ti George. He might find somethin' up there. If he was keen.

BETTY   Ye think so. What y' reckon ti that George?

ANDY   Shields it's knackered...

BETTY   He went for a net makin' job with his pal. Didn' ye George? Y'know, youth opportunities. Huh! he got the sack on the second day, jus' for bein' half an hour late...

ANDY   Did 'e? What aboot his pal?

BETTY   Oh he got the sack on the first day.

ANDY   Oh!

BETTY   Nothin' for them round here... jobwise!
Look at the way he's watchin' that tele. George son! Ye'll ruin yor eyes.
Got that er... thingy...

ANDY   Telescope!

BETTY	Aye! Got it from his nana. Didn't ye George, gerrit from yor nana? She's had it for years... Her husband was lost on a boat called the 'Jeannie Stewart'. Years back... A think it's bad luck keepin' things like that...
ANDY	Lookin' thro' a telescope the wrong way son, makes everythin' seem miles away...
BETTY	George!

(Provocatively he trains the telescope toward them)

GEORGE	Best way isn't it? When yor watchin' rubbish.
BETTY	George!
GEORGE	Was that right about me nana? The' called her Spanish Maria. She was a hoo-a, wasn' she?
BETTY	What sort've thing is that to say.
GEORGE	This owld fella in the Mariners Arms, told us... He'd known her! She was a hoo-a.
BETTY	That's a horrible thing to say. How can ye say a thing like that?
GEORGE	True though! Isn't it?
BETTY	Well, if it is, she was yor bloody father's mother, not mine... So you bear that in mind...
GEORGE	We're all part o' the same set up.
ANDY	That's no way ti talk ti yor muther son!

(GEORGE springs to his feet)

GEORGE	Up yor kilt...

(Saunters to the door)

GEORGE | An' look! If it's so bloody fantastic in Scotland. Why don't ye piss off back...

(Exits)

• • • •

EXT. DAY. THE CULLERCOATS SHORE.

(RAY works at the restoration of his coble. He has the rudder laid on a couple of boxes. GEORGE (Digga), and KEVIN (Grippa) approach. They are having a day at the seaside, and kick a beer can around)

GEORGE | England! England! England! Howway man Grippa, belt it over.
Kick it man! Kick it!

(KEVIN kicks it across. RAY pauses in his work to watch. GEORGE dribbles the can...)

GEORGE | Gasgoine puts it thro' ti Lineker, but Maradonna has nipped in... Comes back again ti Beardesly... Long ball thro' the middle, Gazza picks it up again, dummies round the defence an' wi' that magic left foot...

(He boots the can toward RAY)

GEORGE | It's a goal! Yeh...!

(Leaps and punches the air)

RAY | Hey son...

GEORGE | What?

RAY | Come here!

GEORGE | Who? me?

RAY | Aye!

GEORGE | What for?

RAY	Just a minute…
	(KEVIN closes up to GEORGE)
KEVIN	What's up?
GEORGE	Dunno!
RAY	Come here man!
KEVIN	What's 'e want?
GEORGE	Dunno! What ye want?
RAY	Over here!
GEORGE	We've done nowt…
RAY	Got surplus energy…
GEORGE	Y'what?
KEVIN	Stupid owld gadgy. What's 'e on about?
GEORGE	Yeh! Stupid owld gadgy.
KEVIN	Howway man Digga! Tell 'm to piss off…
RAY	Come here man. Give 's a hand.
KEVIN	Jus' tell 'm ti fuck off. Stupid owld git.
GEORGE	Yeh! Fuck off ye stupid owld git…
RAY	Over here son! C'mon.
GEORGE	Is he deef?
KEVIN	Must be a nutta. Hey! Are ye some sorta nutta? Howway man Digga! Missin' all the tash!
RAY	C'mon lads.
KEVIN	*(Mimicing his teacher)* C'mon lad. Who does 'e

think he is? We're not at school now y'know. "Don' just stand there lad. A'm speakin' ti you lad. Look at me when I'm talkin'."

RAY   Come here!

KEVIN   Is he lookin' for bother?

GEORGE   Aw! see what he wants.

(Strolls over to RAY)

KEVIN   He's a nutta man. Ye want ti watch him.

(GEORGE closes to RAY)

GEORGE   What ye want then?

KEVIN   Digga man!

(RAY hangs on to his wood chisel, but is outside the boat, and vulnerable)

RAY   What's he call ye? Digga?

GEORGE   What about it like?

RAY   Why's he call you that?

GEORGE   'Cos A dig 'm, that's why…

RAY   Oh!

GEORGE   Alright!

RAY   What's it mean then… dig 'm?

GEORGE   A dig 'm. Plant 'm! Knack 'm…

RAY   Oh!

GEORGE   So what ye wantin' eh?

KEVIN   Hey Digga man! Stoppin' here all day or what?

GEORGE   Grippa man! Shut yor hole…

RAY   That his name, Grippa?

GEORGE   What ye shout of us for?

RAY   Wants ti go somewhere does he?

GEORGE   What ye after?

RAY   Where's he want ti go?

GEORGE   A dunno! Majorca! Florida! Disneyland! What
                  about it?

RAY   Never been them places.

                  (*KEVIN wanders over*)

KEVIN   Sorta wreck is this then? Eh?

GEORGE   Fallin' ti bits ain' it!

KEVIN   Yeh! Was for the Tall Ships race, but it shrunk…
                  Yeh! Now it's in for the short arse ships race…

GEORGE   That's right! Then it must've got dry rot.

KEVIN   Worra state!

GEORGE   Torpedoed was it pop?

KEVIN   Yeh! It's a right wreck. Been on the rocks has it
                  pop? Washed up was it?

                  (*Jumps aboard*)

KEVIN   Look at me! A'm friggin' in the riggin'
                  All hands on deck…

                  (*Mocking RAY*)

KEVIN   Cap'n Birds Eye!
                  Abandon ship!
                  Wimmin and children last…

Swim for the shore...

(Dives off. Rolls across the beach)

KEVIN   Save me!

(Grapples with GEORGE)

GEORGE   Grippa, yor friggin' crackers. If brains was dominos ye'd be knockin'...

(Puts KEVIN into a headlock. RAY studies the horseplay)

KEVIN   *(In some pain)* Oya! Oya! Oya!

GEORGE   There's piss comin' outa yor ears!

RAY   Is that the way you talk ti mates...?

GEORGE   *(Releasing KEVIN)* Way A talk ti anybody, OK? What ye gettin' at?

KEVIN   Yeh! What ye gettin' at Cap'n Birds Eye?

GEORGE   What ye wantin'?

RAY   Yor a fit lad. Y'see that. Can ye lift it? *(Points out the rudder)*

GEORGE   What for?

RAY   'Cos it's heavy.

GEORGE   So what?

KEVIN   A could lift that...

GEORGE   Not askin' you stupid. Askin' me.

RAY   Well, could ye?

GEORGE   Might!

KEVIN   Could still lift it...

(GEORGE pushes KEVIN out of the way)

GEORGE   Where ye want it lifted?

RAY   Over the stern post...

KEVIN   That's the back end...

GEORGE   A know that. A'm not ignorant. Not like you. Frig off man Kev, yor in me way...

KEVIN   Shit!

RAY   *(To KEVIN)* Got two names has he?

(GEORGE struggles the rudder up and over the stern post in an impressive display of strength)

RAY   Good lad! That's right! Push it over! Go on! Yor a good'n... Get on board, an' drag it across. That's it. Aye you're a good'n. Well done son! Well done! Smashin'...
That's it. Hey, you've got some beef about ye. Ye handled that right...

(GEORGE suddenly feels important. KEVIN picks up the Tiller Bar)

KEVIN   What's this?

RAY   What y'call the long bar.

KEVIN   The what?

RAY   The long bar! Y' can be thwartship handlin' the throttle, and still keep the helm.

(KEVIN is utterly mystified)

KEVIN   What's 'e talkin' about?

GEORGE   Yor so ignorant Grippa. It's fer the rudder man. Can ye not see?

KEVIN	Alright Ballbrains! Where's the rudder then?
GEORGE	Daft bat! That's what A've just humped on. Pinhead!
KEVIN	Why don't ye fasten it on then. Spasta!
RAY	Cannit put the rudder on yet son.
GEORGE	No good tellin' him man, he's thick.
KEVIN	Friggin' thick you...!
RAY	Goes on the pintles, does the rudder.
KEVIN	Eh?
GEORGE	Cloth ears.
KEVIN	Don' know what he's fuckin' talkin' about.
GEORGE	Look man! He's tellin' ye...
KEVIN	What's the pintles then?
GEORGE	Jus' shown ye has'n 'e. Where the rudder goes... There! Look!
RAY	That's right. But she's got ti be wattered.
KEVIN	(*Exasperated*) What y' mean, wattered?
GEORGE	In the water man. In the water man! 'Cos the rudder goes below the keel...
RAY	That's right son! In fact on a coble it's part o' the keel. Keeps it stable...
GEORGE	Y' see!
RAY	Not everybody would spot that. Ye've got a good eye son...
GEORGE	Brain Grippa! Brains! Ye've got ti have them.

157

KEVIN   Aw frig off! Just a friggin' wreck!

RAY   Well, she's an old boat son. But when A've put her to rights...

GEORGE   Yors is it pop?

RAY   Well, sort of adopted it, y'know!

GEORGE   Puttin' it right are ye?

RAY   Bit by bit!

GEORGE   Gorra engine...?

KEVIN   Loada scrap!

GEORGE   Shut yor friggin' hole Grippa.

RAY   That's an old Morris 11.9. Jus' needs new valves. 'Course she's a sailin' boat originally. A natural sailin' boat.

KEVIN   Oh aye! Where's the friggin' mast then?

RAY   Could get a mast. For the navigation lights. But it doesn't need sail.

GEORGE   Where would ye fit it! The mast?

RAY   There! By the carlin' thoft. For'rd o' the ram.

KEVIN   What's 'e talkin' about. Cannit understand a word he's sayin'.

RAY   The thofts son! Ye have yor fore thoft there, y' see! Then there's the carlin' thoft, that's where the mast goes. Then the foot thoft, an' the after thoft, then ye have the cuddy thoft, which some call the scut.

KEVIN   A've had enough!

RAY   Them clogs, the heavy bits o' wood over the top is fastened there, but the real fastener is the cat band... which comes round the gunnel end...

KEVIN Aw Christ! Howway Digga let's away...

GEORGE Hold on!

KEVIN Talkin' rubbish man! All a fuckin' foreign
language.

RAY *(Remorselessly on)* Now that's the liftin' plank.
What wi call the lower board. If it's saucer wise
lookin' from aft...
Here look... get down... have a look!

(RAY and GEORGE go down to look under the hull)

RAY Y' see! Y'd say that's a stable boat...
'Cos ye can get them standin' up, then they're
coggly...

KEVIN He's a nutta!

GEORGE Coggly?

RAY Means they'll roll... Y' know. *(Demonstrates)*

KEVIN A'm away!

GEORGE Hold on man Grippa! Listen!

RAY Another point is the shoulders! If a boat hasn't
got good shoulders, an' thor's any weather...
she'd get washed out, an' that's what ye call a
dirty bugga.

KEVIN What's 'e talkin' about?

GEORGE A dirty bugga! You should know what that is.

RAY Where you two lads off to then?

GEORGE Along the sands ti Whitley...
Kick a few machines in...
He wants ti go tashin'. All he thinks about.

KEVIN	Listen to the mouth. King o' the Shags!
RAY	Tashin'! What's tashin'?
KEVIN	One up on you pop.
RAY	Tashin'?
KEVIN	Wouldn't do you much good even if wi' explained... heh heh!
RAY	Oh!
KEVIN	Jesus!
RAY	So what di ye do... when yor not tashin'?
GEORGE	Birra hoist! Birra blaggin'.
	(RAYS turn to be mystified...)
KEVIN	Hoist! as in nickin'! Blaggin'! As in smash an' grab. Got ti understand the words pop. Get with it.
RAY	Smash an' grab! What ye do that for?
KEVIN	What for? 'Cos o' the price o' blow! Y' know... the happy baccy!
RAY	Happy baccy?
KEVIN	Where ye been pop? Cannit afford the dog! The broon! The Scottish an' New... Aw! Howway Digga...
	(KEVIN sets off)
GEORGE	What's the boat's name?
RAY	That's something A have to think about. Sort've lost its name. Needs a name.
KEVIN	Digga man. C'mon...

GEORGE	Right! Might see ye then! Might come back this way.
	(Begins to leave)
GEORGE	My Da's a fisherman y' know…
RAY	Is 'e?
GEORGE	Yeh! Been to Iceland… Faroe, Norway… All them places… That's how I knew a bit about what ye were sayin'…
RAY	Fisherman eh!
GEORGE	Aye! So was me Granda! Got his telescope at home.
RAY	Where's yor dad fishin' now?
GEORGE	Well he's like in Spain. I think that's where he's workin' now… in Spain…
RAY	Oh!
GEORGE	Was me Nana give 's the telescope. Brass it is. Got his name on… If ye like A could bring it down ti show ye. Let y' see. Alright pop!
	(Leaves)
RAY	Hey! The name is Ray!
GEORGE	Oh right!
RAY	And… thanks for the lift.
GEORGE	OK. See ye! Oh take no notice o' Grippa, he's just a nutta… Hey Grippa hold on… England! England! England!

• • • •

INT. BEDROOM. MORNING.

*(BETTY in bed with ANDREW. LINDA enters.
Night attire. She begins to search the dressing table.
Deliberately noisy... BETTY raises herself on one
elbow)*

BETTY   What the hell? Linda! What y' doin'?

LINDA   Lookin'...

BETTY   Lookin' for what?

LINDA   Something!

BETTY   Bloody hell! A said, 'Get yor things', last
         night...

LINDA   Didn' know last night...

BETTY   What?

LINDA   Me Tampax! A want me Tampax!

BETTY   Oh fer cryin' out! The second drawer...

         (LINDA noisily rattles the drawer open)

LINDA   Not here...

BETTY   Cris' sake! *(Begins to climb out of bed)* Pass us me
         dressin' gown...

         *(LINDA deliberately hands the gown short so her
         mother has to leave the bed to reach it)*

BETTY   You little sod... you are, our Linda!

         (She hunts through the drawer without success)

BETTY   Where the hell...

         *(ANDREW now fully awake. Eases out the bed. Pulls
         on his underpants, and exits)*

ANDY	Just away ti the yard…
BETTY	*(Finding the towel)* There!
	(LINDA takes them and begins to leave)
BETTY	Linda! There's no need… Linda!
	(LINDA halts)
BETTY	Ye know ye'll always come first.
	(LINDA exits)
ANDY *(O.S)*	Betty! There's nae a bog roll oot here!

• • • •

INT. 'NORTH-SEA SCAMPI LTD'., KNOWN AS SCAMPI JACKS PRAWN FACTORY.

	(The girls in white coats and hats. They are snapping prawns. Removing the body from the head. They gossip as they work. Prawn after prawn, the waste going into a bin, the tails into plastic boxes. The boss SCAMPI JACK is distributing prawns around the benches, making sure the girls keep at it. BETTY arrives, buttoning her coat, and joins NATALIE and EDNA at the bench)
BETTY	Well, that's him away back ti Peterhead. What a week I've put in. Practically at blows. Glad ti back here. Who'd have thought that… snappin' for Scampi Jack…
EDNA	Talk o' the devil…
	(SCAMPI JACK trundles a pile of boxes up to the bench. The women look on disapprovingly)
EDNA	That better not be another load o' beetles.
JACK	Edna, jus' gerron snappin', an' give yor mouth a rest.

EDNA   Not snappin' beetles. Not for one fifty. An' that goes for the rest.

(JACK weighs up the opposition. The women are united)

JACK   Look, there's only ten boxes o' beetles. All the rest is good size. Well have a look! Go on the hourly base if it suits ye.

EDNA   Not the money man! Stood here snappin' that lot! Have ye ever counted them? There's a bastard thousand in every box...

JACK   It's what they're catchin'...

EDNA   Then the' should toss them back.

JACK   They'd just be dead!

EDNA   Rubbish! Call themselves fishermen.

JACK   Edna! Y' know as much about it as John Selwyn Gummer...

EDNA   Who the frig's Selwyn Gummer?

JACK   Another big mouth... *(Trundles off)*

EDNA   Listen here Scampi Jack... There's supposed ti be four lasses on this bench.

JACK   *(Departing)* Edna, A'm sweatin' me balls off.

EDNA   Not be a lot o' steam there then...

NATALIE   Why's Ingrid not turned in?

EDNA   She's upset an' all...

NATALIE   What's upset her?

EDNA   A think she fell down a manhole, an' thor was no men in it...

(They laugh at the thought of the absent INGRID)

EDNA   What were you sayin' Betty?

BETTY   Have I not got a life? That's what I'm wonderin'...

EDNA   Just yorself to blame Betty. If you're soft wi' men, the' push ye over the edge.
A worked at Ocean Foods. Natalie, you'll bear me out. There was this poor lass. Comin' out wi' fifty five quid for a week's graft, an' every Friday mid-day, this shithouse, you remember him Natalie?

NATALIE Oh aye! Right shithouse!

EDNA   Waitin' at the gate ti take it off her.
Left her a quid to get a taxi home. Am I right?

NATALIE Gospel!

BETTY   Andy's good wi' money.

EDNA   Jus' went off, an' pissed it against the wall.

NATALIE Two bairns she had.

EDNA   Bloody shame. Wouldn't care, she thought he was fascinatin'.

NATALIE Good lookin' nowt! Shithouse!

BETTY   Lovely black hair!

EDNA   Eh?

BETTY   Andy! Got lovely black hair. A think that's fascinatin'! Black hair!

(A young man appears at the end of the factory)

NATALIE That looks like the new driver.

BETTY   But our George! Callin' his nan a hoo-a.

165

EDNA	Hey son! Are you the new driver?
NATALIE	Don't recognise him.
EDNA	Gorris pants on that's why.
BETTY	A mean, A thought it was terrible that. Callin' his nan a cow. Maybe she was. But A mean… It was like there was more to it.
EDNA	Hey son! Drop yor pants, see if wi recognise ye…
BETTY	A mean, A know he's havin' a bad time. A know he cannit gerra job. A would like him ti make somethin' of himself. He wasn't that bad at school.
EDNA	*(Losing interest in the driver)* I blame the schools. An' the schools blame the parents.
BETTY	Cannit understand.
EDNA	Ye go up ti the school. What's the point?
NATALIE	Eee! A was dead thick at school. Teachers hated me.
EDNA	Who would the' find ti do this stupid work?
NATALIE	Work in a fish house, the' think yor common.
EDNA	But if we pack in, the fishin' 's finished here. What do teachers know about that?
NATALIE	Who's Selwyn Gummer anyhow? Is it a man?
EDNA	Can 'e snap beetles?

• • • •

THE SHORE.

(RAY is working on his boat. He saws timber for deck planks. Rests. Takes out his tea flask GEORGE comes over the bankside. Approaching casual. Diffident)

RAY	Alright?
GEORGE	Hello Ray. Alright yourself?
RAY	Alright!
GEORGE	Good! Just passin'…
RAY	Aye!

(GEORGE saunters round the boat)

GEORGE	How's it goin' then?
RAY	Not bad.
GEORGE	Gettin' on with it eh?
RAY	Oh aye!
GEORGE	Bit more done eh?
RAY	That's right!
GEORGE	Good!
RAY	Where's yor pal then?
GEORGE	Grippa!
RAY	That's the one.
GEORGE	On the bank top.
RAY	Oh!

(RAY pours his tea)

GEORGE	Havin' a crap!

(RAY reflects into his tea cup. Discards it)

RAY	Oh!
GEORGE	This new plankin'?

RAY

That's right! Oak! Like iron!
Takes some cuttin'.

GEORGE

Aye! It will do. *(Produces his telescope)* What ye
think o' that then?
(RAY examines it)

RAY

'George Peason, 1825'. That's an old 'n. Where
ye get that?

GEORGE

Was tellin' ye! Was me Da's.

RAY

That's right. Ye was tellin' me.

GEORGE

That's my name that. George Pearson!

RAY

Is that right! *(Glances thro' it)* Good glass.

GEORGE

Yeh!

(RAY hands it back)

RAY

Has he come back then?

GEORGE

Come back?

RAY

Ye were sayin! Yor Da! He'd gone away. Spain
wasn't it?

GEORGE

No! He's not come back.

RAY

Crazy! Spain! We sell 'm Shield's trawlers.
Then Shield's men have ti go an' work there, so
the' can fish British waters.

GEORGE

EEC or somethin' isn't it?

RAY

Same boats. Same men. Laid up here.

GEORGE

Yeh!

RAY

Politics! Cod War was the same. You'll not
remember. Thousands on the scrapheap!
Hull! Grimsby... Families broke up!
Two hundred mile limit! Ye bugga!

'Poor little Iceland, it's all they've got'.
Used ti go on about landowners. Now they've
got sea owners.
Might as well say, 'poor Duke o' Northumberland, all he's got is the North of England...'
Politicians! A think the Yanks had somethin' ti
do wi' that. Somethin' up there the' wanted.

GEORGE   What ye make o' Scotsmen then?

RAY   Was never welcome in Shields. Now the' cannit
                do without them.

GEORGE   A don't like 'm much... Scotties!

RAY   Alright! Superstitious buggas! Never sail on
                Fridays, or if the' see a nun...!

GEORGE   That's crackers...

                (*KEVIN appears on the bank top. They watch him
                make his way down*)

RAY   I've never seen a nun on Shield's Fish Quay.

GEORGE   Gorra one stayin' with us...

RAY   A nun?

GEORGE   Naw! A scottie!

RAY   Oh! I knew a one! Used to go round the deck
                with a burnin' rag on the end of a pole... Burnin'
                out the evil spirits...

GEORGE   Gerron!

RAY   S'fact! Did no bloody good like... Little buggas
                jus' run up the mast...

                (*He nudges GEORGE. It's a leg pull. GEORGE sees
                the joke. They are becoming close. KEVIN joins
                them*)

RAY   Talkin' of evil spirits. You alright son?

169

KEVIN	Aye!
	(Subdued. He sits on the sand. Their oulines assume the 'Boyhood of Raleigh')
RAY	Feelin' better? On the pop were ye?
KEVIN	Could be.
RAY	Tashin'?
KEVIN	Jokin'.
GEORGE	When ye've got this ready. What's the plan?
KEVIN	Aye! When's the world cruise Ray?
RAY	Comin' as passenger?
KEVIN	Jus' cancelled me bookin'…
GEORGE	Gonna sell it… are ye?
RAY	Naw! Fishin'! Take'n it out fishin'…
KEVIN	Couldn't go fishin' in that.
RAY	That's a good boat.
GEORGE	Too small man!
RAY	*(Pointing seaward)* Sou' by Sou' East, right! With a boat this size, A've come back with a hundred fish.
KEVIN	Sorta fish?
RAY	Salmon, grilse, sea trout. Huh! Like bars o' silver. Sold'm for shillin's. Naw! This sorta boat is the same as what brought the Vikin's. Now Danes! There's fishermen I've time for. Talk about small. A Dane could sail a fish box over the North Sea. Aye! An' fetch it back full o' haddocks…

170

(Takes up his saw, and resumes work)

RAY   All this obsession wi' bigger, more powerful boats. Where's it got them? What's done?
Great purse nets, two miles long. Skippers sittin' in padded armchairs. Beamers, ploughin' the sea bed. Look at Shields! Where's the cod gone? Where's the herrin' gone?
No. Smalls got ti come back one day. Got ti give the fish a chance. Let them grow!
Well! You two just gonna sit there, or are ye gonna give us a hand?

● ● ● ●

SCAMPI JACK's.

(Time as before. Girls work on. Prawn after Prawn)

EDNA   Scampi! Ye bugga!

NATALIE   Scampi Jack! Wants lockin' up.

EDNA   Comin' out that mincer like shitty toothpaste...

NATALIE   If the' could see what they're eatin'.

EDNA   Serves 'm right! Greedy bastards!
Scampi! Took the grub out the mouth o' the workin' class...
A can remember! You'll not remember!

NATALIE   Here wi go! Not the good old days again!

EDNA   A can remember when prawns was hot, fresh and boiled.
My mother...

NATALIE   boiled 'em in the wash house set pot...

EDNA   That's right! Handful o' salt! Tang o' the Sunlight soap! Lush!

NATALIE   Here wi go!

171

EDNA	Tellin' ye. Only ever got sold in Shields, Wallsend, Byker. Places like that. Upper classes thought eatin' prawns was like eatin' frogs… Ye could go…
NATALIE	Ti old man Vasey's fish shop in Frederick Street…
EDNA	Now listen… For ninepence, ye got as many as ye could wrap up in the Newcastle Chronicle… and I'm talkin' about prawns… y' know.

(Demonstates an exaggerated size)

EDNA	Y'bugga, ye cannit even buy the bloody Chronicle for that now…
BETTY	Things change. Everybody can remember better times. But were the'?
NATALIE	Talkin' ti that lad. The new driver…
EDNA	Are ye humpin' him?
NATALIE	D'ye mind?
EDNA	A wouldn't mind…
NATALIE	He was a designer in the drawin' office at Swan Hunters… Sad that innit? Endin' up here with us…
BETTY	What can ye do?
EDNA	Did y' see Andy this dinner time?

• • • •

THE LOUNGE BAR OF THE MARINER'S ARMS.

(BETTY comes in to a table. ANDREW follows bringing the drinks. He sits)

BETTY	Ta!

ANDY   What ye've tae realise Betty. He's lookin' fer an excuse tae his ain inadequacy.

BETTY   Andy man! Can wi' not just have a quiet drink?

ANDY   Tryin' ti dominate ye. His life is a mess, so he wants tae make a mess o' yors...

BETTY   Cannit stop long. A've ti get back on shift.

ANDY   He's like a stone around yor neck.

BETTY   A know. A know the problem Andy.

ANDY   He'll take ye doon wirrim!

BETTY   Are ye wantin' away Andy?

ANDY   A could take care o' ye... ye know that!

(Pause. BETTY doesn't know if it is even worth pretending to a belief in it. But it might be true...)

BETTY   When ye sailin'?

ANDY   Tonight! A think we're aff tae the North Bank. Probably a five day trip.
We're sure tae land in Eyemouth at the weekend.
If ye fancied a couple o' days up there, it'd make a break fer ye.
What'd ye say?

BETTY   Maybe, when ye get back ti Shields, we'll get somethin' sorted out.

ANDY   Betty man! Ye keep puttin' aff... It's a straight choice. Ye cannit live someone else's life.

BETTY   Eee! What time is it?

ANDY   *(Consulting his watch)* Twenty past!

BETTY   Eeee! An' A'm sittin' here.

173

ANDY	Fer cryin' out. Finish yor drink.
BETTY	*(Half in. Half out her chair)* A've promised our Linda. Ti get her some crab sticks.

(ANDY gives up)

• • • •

SCAMPI JACK's.

(The girls are clearing up. Putting on their outdoor clothing. Time to go home)

EDNA	We are all waitin' for our ship ti come in Betty...
BETTY	A'm watchin' mine sail away... A mean, is it too much to ask for people ti be reasonable?
EDNA	Y' know what bein' reasonable gets ye.
NATALIE	*(Weighing off the last of the prawns)* All the bloody beetles...
BETTY	Why should it be so complicated? A just want a share...
EDNA	Kids! Can be full o' love, but the' draw the line at sharin'... Just blurt thing out Betty! Well that's what A do. Bottle it up for so long, then A have a bloody good blurt.
BETTY	A tell ye how it's gettin'. Up ti here.
EDNA	'Course ye could always go out, an' get pissed.
BETTY	A'm not lookin' for the bright lights Edna.
NATALIE	Wouldn't find 'em round here. Shields! It's dead!
EDNA	Aw when yor pissed, even Shields can look like Piccadilly Circus.

174

BETTY	If A could get them ti understand…
EDNA	Then have a blurt Betty. Have a bloody good blurt.

• • • •

THE LIVING ROOM.

(GEORGE comes in. Preparing to go out, lacing up his boots. Combs his hair. His mother enters. He is aware of her but does not turn around. She hangs up her coat. Underneath, the white smock of the factory)

BETTY	Goin' out then? Time will ye be back?
GEORGE	Dunno!
BETTY	Jus' 'cos A might be out mesel'.

(GEORGE shrugs his indifference)

BETTY	So, if I am, there's ham in the fridge, y' can make yorsel' a sandwich.

(GEORGE turns from the mirror)

BETTY	Aw George! Ye've got them filthy jeans on again, an' ye've got a wardrobe o' clean ones. Ye'd think ye had nowt ti wear.

(GEORGE begins to leave)

BETTY	Listen!

(He stops. Keeps his back to her)

BETTY	We've got ti get somethin' sorted.
GEORGE	A'm late!
BETTY	Where ye goin'?
GEORGE	Out!

BETTY A was thinkin' of takin' a week-end away.
A don't want ye gettin' into any bother... you
an' Linda...
So A'll leave ye stocked up.
George, fer Cris' sake will ye look at us...
If ye don't look at us how can A tell if yor
listenin'?
George! A'm yor mother! All A want is for wi all
ti be happy. But! A bit o' happiness for mesel'...
George! Ye never even ask us how I am!...

GEORGE *(Without looking around)* How are ye?

(He leaves)

BETTY *(Calling after him)* Ye never knew what A put up
with from yor Da.
Ye had no idea.
When he left me, A was never so glad ti see the
back o' anybody.

• • • •

THE BEACH.

*(GRIPPA with a saw is resting. Listening to RAY.
RAY is demonstrating on the sand the technique of
line fishing. GEORGE comes over. He seems down-
cast. Takes up hammer and nails. Gets to work on the
point of the coble. RAY spears the sand with a pole)*

RAY The Dan! Yor marker! Right! If it's a flood tide,
flowin' from where you are... right!

(Draws on the sand with a stick)

RAY Got ti put in more tow, on the end tow, for when
the tide ebbs, so the Dan keeps above water...
So! Ye've got excess tow, right!

(GRIPPA is mystified)

RAY So the tide is knockin' yor Dan!
If a man comes round the tide side, he's gettin'
involved with all that slack... gerrit!

176

RAY   *(Aside to GEORGE)* Alright George?

       (Again to GRIPPA) Before ye can be a fisherman
       son, ye've got ti be a seaman.
       Runnin' in to a lee shore, an' the seas up yor arse.
       Ye've got ti see things afore the' happen...

       (GRIPPA cannot mentally cope...)

RAY   I dunno! What the hell di' the' teach you lads at
       school?

       (To GEORGE) Hey! Is them nails copper, or
       galvanized?

GEORGE   Copper!

RAY   That's alright then. But move that timber back.
       She's got ti be trim. Every little bit! Throttle back,
       the heed comes up! We'd be brayin' into the sea.

GEORGE   *(Stops working)* The talk in Shields is... no fish.

RAY   Now A'll tell ye! The' murdered the sprats.
       Every boat outa Shields dredgin' sprats.
       Year in, year out. An' fer what?
       Fertiliser! Now they're fished out, so they're
       moanin'... 'Where's the cod gone?'
       Ye murder the sprats, ye murder the cod.
       That's what big boats is about.
       Senseless, bloody destructive greed...
       Think the' didn't have sons or gran'sons.
       Wi small boats, yor closer ti the water.

GEORGE   If there's no fish Ray, what's the point?

RAY   The sea! It's like yor muther! Ye can treat her badly,
       she's still gonna feed ye. She'll come back...

GEORGE   Ye can get a machine now for baitin' hooks.
       Was in the 'Fishin' News'.

RAY   Forget it! Need a lot more'n a baitin' machine.
       Wi need a mast! Navigation lights! Rope, sea
       anchor, battery!

	First things first…
GEORGE	Can get grants for all that sorta thing. Off the EEC or somethin'.
RAY	That'd be the day…
GEORGE	Wi could ask… Could always ask…
RAY	A know what they'd say…
KEVIN	Aye! Fuck off!
GEORGE	No man! Wi should give it a go.

(RAY picks up his mallet and chisel and works on)

RAY	A've seen a thirty stone halibut caught on a long line… There was feedin' on it for four hundred. A single fish. We sold in Shields for a shillin' a pound. A've got a photo of it somewhere. No man! Ye've got ti let things grow.

• • • •

INT. DAY. THE OFFICE OF THE MINISTRY OF AGRICULTURE AND FISHERIES, NORTH SHIELDS.

(A young girl secretary is alone in the office. Enter GEORGE and KEVIN. The girl stops typing)

SECRETARY	Can I help you?
GEORGE	This the office?
SECRETARY	What is it you wanted?
GEORGE	Just a word wi' somebody.
SECRETARY	What connection?
GEORGE	It's about grants.

KEVIN	For fishin' boats
GEORGE	Well, just a small one.
KEVIN	So we'll only want a small grant.
SECRETARY	I'm afraid the principal officer is out.
KEVIN	By yorsel' are ye… pet!
SECRETARY	Not sure when he'll be back.
GEORGE	Just wanted some general info.
KEVIN	So you'll probably do.
GEORGE	There's this boat y' see.
KEVIN	Like wi' say… just a small boat.
GEORGE	Needs a few bits an' pieces.
KEVIN	Not a lot.
GEORGE	So we're wonderin'… er!
KEVIN	How ti go on.
GEORGE	If there is any…
KEVIN	thing going…
GEORGE	In the way of er… y' know…
KEVIN	Money!
SECRETARY	If you'd like to leave your names.
GEORGE	Well it's not fer us y' see…
KEVIN	No! It's fer a mate of ours. Y' know…
SECRETARY	It's not your boat?
GEORGE	No! It belongs this blokee!

179

KEVIN	He's called Ray! Strite up! It's not hoisty, or nowt like that.
SECRETARY	Is the boat registered?
	(KEVIN begins to wander about the office investigating the shelves)
GEORGE	Is it what?
SECRETARY	Registered! With a fishing number.
KEVIN	*(Sub voce)* Just say yes!
GEORGE	Yes!
SECRETARY	With Customs and Excise?
GEORGE	Y' what?
KEVIN	Oh we are accustomed ti exercise! Eh! Just a joke... y' know!
SECRETARY	Because if it is not renewed annually, the Registry expires.
KEVIN	Does it?
GEORGE	No we didn't know that.
SECRETARY	So who holds the current certificate?
GEORGE	'Spect Ray will have that.
KEVIN	Oh aye! 'Spect so!
SECRETARY	What is the name of the boat?
GEORGE	Oh he hasn't decided about that yet.
SECRETARY	It's a new boat is it?
KEVIN	Not exactly.
GEORGE	No, it's not quite new.

SECRETARY	Is it a boat that is being reconditioned?
	(Pause)
KEVIN	No! We are just doin' it up.
GEORGE	*(Hastily)* Not that we're gettin' paid or nowt, like…
KEVIN	No. There's no skin off the Nash.
GEORGE	No. Don't get the idea. No cashers!
KEVIN	What ye call a love job. Y' know what A mean?
SECRETARY	Is it a boat that has been de-commissioned?
GEORGE	I'm sure if there was anythin' wanted doin' on it. Ray would see to it.
KEVIN	Definitely!
GEORGE	Very thorough.
KEVIN	Look! Is there not any forms?
GEORGE	Yeah! Mus' be some proper forms.
KEVIN	Always is…
	(Secretary takes a form from a cabinet)
SECRETARY	Well, there is this, it's an Explanatory leaflet.
KEVIN	That'd be good…
SECRETARY	Concerns the FEOGA grants dealt with by the SIFA.
GEORGE	Who is the SIFA?
SECRETARY	Well they replaced the old HIB and WFA.
KEVIN	Did the'…?

SECRETARY	Here we are. Form F21 double AS. Regulation EEC…
KEVIN	That's it. The EEC. That'll be the one.
SECRETARY	Construction of, and modernisation of Fishing Vessels, and the development of Aquaculture.
GEORGE	Aquaculture?
KEVIN	Thought that was stickin' pins in people.
SECRETARY	Section one, section two… yes! Vessels must be between nine and thirty metres, between the perpendiculars.
GEORGE	Perpendiculars?
SECRETARY	Possessing the necessary equipment for fishing operation, and crew safetly. Section four… Projects for modernisation must be substantial, undertaken to rationalise…
KEVIN	Rationalise?
SECRETARY	Etc. etc…
KEVIN	Is there an explanatory leaflet for the explanatory leaflet?
SECRETARY	While the sterling equivalent may change marginally, the total cost of the project must be at least 20,000 ECUs…
GEORGE	What's an ECU?
SECRETARY	European currency!
KEVIN	So what's 20,000 o' them?
SECRETARY	The minimum cost. Approximately £12,000.
KEVIN	Y' what? Twelve thoosand poond! Hey! We'll sell ye the boat fer that.

SECRETARY	Is she under nine metres?
	(KEVIN and GEORGE are not sure what nine metres is)
SECRETARY	Twenty nine feet!
	(They think about it)
KEVIN	Wi could always... like y' know... stick a bit on...
GEORGE	Twenty nine feet?
SECRETARY	Yes! Between the...
KEVIN	Porpendiculars! Aye! Wi got that bit.
GEORGE	Are ye sayin' we're too small?
SECRETARY	I'm sorry. Maybe if you come back to see...
GEORGE	The principal officer!
SECRETARY	He is the...
GEORGE	It's alright pet. Wi get the message. Nowt here for us, is there?
SECRETARY	I'm very sorry...
GEORGE	Not your fault. Don' worry. Howway Grippa, we're not big enough... *(Leaves)*
KEVIN	Alright pet! We'll just have ti consult with wor accountants on the next step. Tirra!
	(Pausing)
KEVIN	Hey! If A was a principal officer, A wouldn't leave you here on yor own.
	(GEORGE turns back and hauls KEVIN out the office)

• • • •

THE BEACH. THE COBLE. AM.

> (*RAY comes carrying his tool bag and a wrapped board...*
> *Setting down his tools. He unwraps the board, and sets it against the prow of the coble...*
> *He has painted a name for the boat... in lavish scroll... 'George Pearson'...*
> *A blanketed head pops over the gunnel.*
> *Taken by surprise RAY hurriedly covers the name board...*
> *GEORGE appears from under the blanket arousing himself from sleep*)

GEORGE   Alright Ray? (*Standing*) Canny mornin'.

RAY   You been sleepin' in there?

GEORGE   Why aye! No bother.

RAY   Man ye'll be stiff as a board.

GEORGE   A've slept rougher! Ye want to try a strip cell.
Hey! That air smells great.
Grippa! Stir yorsel'...

> (*GRIPPA rises up from the depth of the boat.*
> *His blanket is marked 'property of Blyth Marina'*)

KEVIN   Ray! Hey me throat's like a badger's arse...

GEORGE   Shift!

> (*GEORGE bends down, and hoists an aluminium yacht's mast into the vertical. It is replete with navigation lights*)

GEORGE   What y' think o' that then Ray?

RAY   Where the hell did ye get that?

GEORGE   On the job man! Me an' Grippa picked it up... good eh!

RAY   Picked it up? Where?

GEORGE   Just picked it up. No fears steady men!
                Will it fit?
                We'll need a bit 'U' iron for the base.

RAY   Fit where?

GEORGE   *(Mimicing RAY's accent)* By the carlin' thoft!
                For'rd o' the Ram. Where the mast gans. Yahooo!
                (He holds it in position)

RAY   Whose is it?

GEORGE   Whose was it!

RAY   Y'what?

GEORGE   An' what about the lights man?
                Y'see, green, red, white. An' look we've got a
                battery.
                Grippa give's a hand here.
                Fasten them crocodile clips on…
                Go on man. Stick 'm on!

                (The lights on the mast illuminate… Flicker)

GEORGE   Tried 'em last night. Worked perfect!

                (They come on steadily)

GEORGE   There y' are! How's that. Yahoooo!

KEVIN   Great eh! An' looka this…

                *(He heaves over a succession of life jackets… Hauls
                up an anchor…)*

KEVIN   Looka this! Anchors away! Got the lot man Ray.

                *(They hang fenders over the side. A marker buoy, a
                chernokeef log)*

KEVIN   Dunno what the hell this is!

                *(A boathook. KEVIN dons an American admirals
                cap)*

GEORGE	An' look at this. Look Ray! Grippa give 's a hand here!
	(They lift over the gunnel a cylinder life raft, and jump down onto the beach beside it)
KEVIN	How about that?
RAY	*(Recovering)* Do yous know what that is? That's a life raft! A bloody life raft.
KEVIN	Is it? *(To GEORGE)* There y' are! I told you it would be useful. A thought it was somethin' important...
RAY	Where ye get all this?
KEVIN	Blyth.
RAY	Blyth!
KEVIN	Good place Blyth. Got a lot goin' for it. Tons o' stuff up there...
RAY	Ye've bloody pinched this...
KEVIN	Could go back no bother...
RAY	Bloody pinched!
KEVIN	Now hang on Ray. Don't go spare!
RAY	You can bloody get this lot away. The lot!
KEVIN	Hold on man!
RAY	Now A'm tellin' ye. A want this away. Now!
KEVIN	Hey man! What's up? It's all the things wi need.
RAY	Just gerrit away. Ye've took 'm off people's boats. Other people's boats... You bloody little sods.

KEVIN

Man! Them's people as can afford it. Thor goin' round in pleasure boats. Sailin' for fun. It means nowt ti them.

RAY

Is that so! Well it might be nowt ti them, an' it might be nowt ti you, but it's summick ti me. Just get it away!

GEORGE

Ye said wi needed a sea anchor, a mast, lights.

KEVIN

Couldn't get the compass. Got a one a bit loosened, but it wouldn't come off the bulkhead...

RAY

Shift it! Shift it now!

KEVIN

Look man Ray.

RAY

Bloody shift it. An' then the pair o' ye... bugga off!

KEVIN

It was all just stuff lyin' around.

RAY

No bloody argument. Get it shifted.

KEVIN

Christ! He's blown a fuse. Cannit believe it. Losin' his blob.
Ye gone insane or summit? Ray man!

RAY

Just bloody shift it.

KEVIN

Aw frig it! Ray yor crackers. We was up half the night for this lot...
Jesus! No point arguin'...

(Leaves grumbling) Gorra find another van now! Bastard!

(They watch him go. GEORGE throws his blanket disgustedly into the boat)

GEORGE

There was no other way! Wi didn't do it for ourselves. Wi did it fer you.

RAY

I am not havin'...

GEORGE   (*Angry*) Fer you Ray. That's who wi did it for…

RAY   Have you any idea. Have ye? Di you realise what a life raft is.

             (*He grabs GEORGE*)

RAY   Somebody at sea, ye daft little sod! Somebody at sea, could be at risk, dependin' on somethin' you've bloody well nicked… Di ye not care?

GEORGE   Who cares about us Ray?

RAY   Oh aye! Is that yor answer? Lad have ye no sense? Can ye not see the stupidity?
             What the hell is wrong wi' you young'ens?
             Yor lost! Ye don' give a damn…

GEORGE   An' who give's a damn about us?

RAY   Did nobody ever tell ye anythin'?
             At school. At yor home?

GEORGE   Oh aye! The' told us plenty. Nobody will ever give ye anythin'! Ye have to go out an' gerrit for yoursel'… That's what we got told.

RAY   On the sea! Out there!

             (*He forces GEORGE to look*)

RAY   Look! Look at it! There's too much at stake. People have to work together. With respect. Cannit claw off each other's backs. It won't work that way.
             Not out there.
             What would yor Da say? Eh! If he knew.
             What would he say, when he comes home eh? What's he gonna think? His son, a fisherman's son, pulling a stunt like this.
             Di ye not care!
             Di ye not care about his name?

(He releases GEORGE, and hands him the name plate he has engraved. GEORGE is emotionally caught up. Takes it)

GEORGE   Doesn't matter does it!

RAY   Doesn't matter?

GEORGE   'Cos he's not comin' home. Not now. Not ever. So it doesn't matter.

(Puts down the board)

GEORGE   Was fer you Ray! A thought ye would've been pleased. A thought ye would've said, 'Great' 'Smashin', 'Well done'.

RAY   Ye expected me ti say that?

GEORGE   Ray man! A was startin' ti feel like it was great comin' down here.
Like it was where A belonged. Now it's all pissed up.

RAY   You want ti get a few things sorted out in yor head, expectin' me ti say that.
Huh!... well done!

GEORGE   Yor the only one... ever has...

RAY   What you lookin' for?

(GEORGE abruptly leaves)

• • • •

INT. THE LIVING ROOM. EARLY MORNING.

(Enter LINDA. Wearing a slip. Goes to mirror and brushes her hair. Enter BETTY. Putting on her coat)

BETTY   Just away down ti the shop. A'll get some bacon an' milk.

LINDA   Uh huh!

BETTY	What ye do with it! Could do with a herd o' cows in this house, the way ye's sup it.
	(ANDY enters. Reading the morning paper. Tousled. Shirt and braces. Lounges in the big chair)
LINDA	Mam!
BETTY	What?
LINDA	Get some rice crispies!
	(Adjusts her bra. ANDY lowers his paper the better to observe)
BETTY	A bloody well will not!
LINDA	Aw Ma!
BETTY	Yor gettin' like a pig our Linda, A'll not be two minutes. *(Leaves)*
	(Through the mirror, LINDA becomes away of ANDY's interest. She pauses in the brushing of her hair. ANDY returns his gaze to the paper, and considers an opening remark)
ANDY	Mind! I sometimes wonder where ye put it.
LINDA	Pardon?
ANDY	Ye've a healthy appetite!
	(Lowers his paper. Studies her)
ANDY	Nothin' wrong wi' a healthy appetite!
	(LINDA resumes brushing)
ANDY	So lang as you're in good shape. It's good tae see a young lassie, wi' an interest in her appearance. Aw! Ye mind me o' me sister! She brushed her hair, two hun'red times every mornin'.

Counted every stroke.
It shone like glass.
Aye! Lookin' at you Linda, A could wish A were
a handsome young laddie again.

LINDA   *(Stopping brushing to turn and look at him)* How
old are ye?

ANDY   Och! What sorta question is that?

LINDA   Are ye as old as me Da?

ANDY   Di ye think A'm as old as yor Da?

LINDA   *(Turning back to the mirror)* What shoulda call ye?

ANDY   What's wrong wi' Andy! Jus' call me Andy.

LINDA   A think A'd better call ye Uncle Andrew.

ANDY   Uncle Andrew! That's no too bad.
Maybe A could be yor favourite uncle.

LINDA   Uncle Billy was me favourite uncle.

ANDY   Oh! Didn't know ye had an Uncle Billy.

LINDA   We haven't... now!

ANDY   Oh!

LINDA   He used ti give George an' me a pound each,
when he came ti see Ma.

ANDY   That a fact?

LINDA   'Course A was only fourteen at the time, so A
suppose a pound seemed like a lot of money.

ANDY   It would!
That was your Uncle Billy eh! Where's ye Uncle
Billy the noo?

LINDA   Dunno! A think he had ti go away, 'cos somebody was lookin' for 'm.

ANDY	Oh!
LINDA	Maybe you'll do the same…
ANDY	Maybe!
LINDA	Eee! A couldn't brush me hair two hundred times, me arms would be achin'.
ANDY	Ye should let somebody do it for you then…

(Puts down his paper. Closes to her)

ANDY	Here gi' us the brush.

(She hesitates. Then hands him the brush without looking around. He begins to brush her hair. GEORGE enters the room. At the threshold of the door he takes in the scene. He is carrying the telescope)

ANDY	A'm no hurtin' A'm A…? There! Does that feel alright? Does that feel nice?
GEORGE	You bastard!

(LINDA snatches the brush from ANDY)

ANDY	Hey! What's up wi' you?
LINDA	Ee! Yor gonna get yor hammers you are. Out all night again.
GEORGE	Get yor friggin' hands off her.
ANDY	Now you just watch it laddie…
GEORGE	Haggis shit!
LINDA	Mam's gonna tell you what for.
GEORGE	Go an' get yor claes on…
LINDA	Don' you tell me…

GEORGE   Gerrout!

LINDA   Now you just stop it our George.

GEORGE   Come here you.

ANDY   Now look son. Just calm down!
              A'm tellin' ye.

GEORGE   You! tellin' me...

LINDA   George, don't you dare...

GEORGE   You bastard...

              (GEORGE lunges. But ANDY kicks him in the groin,
              and GEORGE reels away. Linda screaming is strug-
              gling with ANDY. GEORGE recovering from the
              blow, fells ANDREW with a blow from the telescope.
              LINDA runs screaming from the house. ANDREW
              trying to regain his feet, is struck down again)

                    • • • •

        EXT. DAY. THE LOW NEWTON REMAND CENTRE.

              (Int. A cell. Bunk, locker, jug, potty. GEORGE
              reclines on the bunk. Off Stage The wing chorus that
              greets a new arrival)

(O.S)   *(A rhythmic banging on the pipes Bang! Bang!*
              Bang!)

CON (O.S)   No.5! You that's just come in.

(O.S)   *(Bang! Bang! Bang!)*

CON (O.S)   No.5! Come ti yor door... *(Pause)*

(O.S)   *(Bang! Bang! Bang!)*

CON (O.S)   You that's just come in, come ti yor door.
              Y' there? No.5. Identify!

(O.S)   *(Bang! Bang! Bang!)*

GEORGE	*(To himself)* Piss off!
(O.S)	*(Bang! Bang! Bang!)*
CON *(O.S)*	No.5. Who are ye? Where ye from?
	(Bang! Bang! Bang! GEORGE picks up the potty, and strikes the door)
GEORGE	A'm GBH. From Hell on Earth, an' A said piss off!
	(Pause. Then the rhythmic banging begins again)
(O.S)	*(Bang! Bang! Bang!)*
CON *(O.S)*	Who are ye? Where ye from? No.5!
GEORGE	Get lost!
CON *(O.S)*	Some fuckin' bottle eh! Who are ye? Where ye from No 5?
(O.S)	*(Bang! Bang! Bang!)*
	Come ti yor door… You a forty three? You a nonce?
(O.S)	*(Bang! Bang! Bang!)*
CON *(O.S)*	We got a beast on the wing. Beast on the wing.
	(Echoing down the wing. The inmates take up the chorus)
(O.S)	Beast! Beast! Beast! Beast! Beast!
CON *(O.S)*	You a grass? You a screw's backside No.5…
	(The prison officer intervenes)
P. OFFICER *(O.S)*	Alright! Alright! Pack it in you bastards. One minute to lights out! Hit your pits.

(Silence. Pause…)

(O.S)	*(Bang! Bang! Bang!)*

CON *(O.S)*   Come slop out No.5. Yor gonna get yor fuckin'
head kicked in.

(O.S)   *(Bang! Bang! Bang!)*

CON *(O.S)*   Got no mammy! Got no daddy! Just the bogey
in the alley. No.5. You get funny dreams in here
No.5. Who are ye? Where ye from… No.5!
Gonna put yor head in the piss pot!

(GEORGE defiantly pounds back on his cell door)

GEORGE   Geordie Pearson!
From Shields! An' listen, I can walk on water…
Geordie Pearson… Shield's boy!
And I got a boat with my name on it.
Listen yous!
I can gut fish, an' read the stars.
Geordie Pearson… from Shields!
Put me in an iron box, an' A'll sail it round the
world…
Come on then! Come on!

(The lights dim and go out)

GEORGE   A don't hear you moanin'!
'Cos even in the dark. In the fuckin' black dark.
A can hear the sea.
And in the mornin'. I'll be here!
Geordie Pearson! Boy from Shields!
Will be around… in the mornin'…

The End

The Playwright

Tom Hadaway was born in the dockside area of North Shields, and he was already more than forty when he began to write stories for radio. He moved to drama when encouraged by the late playwright C.P. Taylor.

Hadaway's television work includes BBC Play for The Day, *The Happy Hunting Ground*, *God Bless Thee Jackie Maddison* (directed by Jack Gold and the BBC-BAFTA entry) and a *Sea Tales and Country Tales* series for BBC Bristol. He also wrote the first series of *When the Boat Comes in* with Sid Chaplin and Alex Glasgow, and has had a long association with Newcastle's Live Theatre Company, who stage premiered all three of the plays published here.

IRON Press was formed in Spring 1973, initially to publish the magazine IRON which more than two decades, and more than 1,500 writers on, survives as one of the country's most active alternative mags – a fervent purveyor of new poetry, fiction and graphics. £10.00 gets you a subscription. Try our intriguing book list too, titles which can rarely be found on the shelves of mega-stores. Fortified by a belief in good writing, as against literary competitions or marketing trivia, IRON remains defiantly a small press. Our address is on the second page of this book.